Acanthus Press Reprint Series
The 19th Century: Landmarks in Design
Volume II

John Hall
and the Grecian Style
in America

Acanthus Press Reprint Series
The 19th Century: Landmarks in Design
Volume II

John Hall
and the Grecian Style
in America

*A reprint of three pattern books
published in 1840 with an illustrated
essay by Thomas Gordon Smith.*

The Cabinet Makers' Assistant

A Series of Select and
Original Modern Designs for
Dwelling Houses

A New and Concise Method
of Hand-Railing

ACANTHUS PRESS 1996

Acanthus Press wishes to thank the following institutions for their assistance in the production of this volume:
The Winterthur Library, Winterthur, Delaware, for allowing us to reproduce their copies of *The Cabinet Makers' Assistant* and *A Series of Select and Original Modern Designs for Dwelling Houses*; and
University of Delaware Library, Newark, Delaware, for allowing us to reproduce their copy of *A New and Concise Method of Hand-Railing*.

Library of Congress Cataloging–in–Publication Data

Hall, John, b. 1809 or 10.
    John Hall and the Grecian style in America : A reprint of three pattern books published in 1840 / with an illustrated essay by Thomas Gordon Smith.
        p. cm. — (Acanthus Press reprint series. The 19th century, landmarks in design ; v. 2)
    First work originally published: The cabinet makers' assistant. Baltimore: J. Murphy, 1840; 2nd work originally published: A series of select and original modern designs for dwelling houses. Baltimore: J. Murphy, 1840; 3rd work originally published: A new and concise method of hand-railing. Baltimore: J. Murphy, 1840.
    Includes bibliographical references (p.   ).
    ISBN 0-926494-06-6 (hc : alk. paper)
    1. Cabinetwork. 2. Hand-railing. 3. Architecture, Domestic—Designs and plans.
I. Smith, Thomas Gordon, 1948. II. Hall, John, b. 1809 or 10. Cabinet makers' assistant.
III. Hall, John, b. 1809 or 10. Series of select and original modern designs for dwelling houses. IV. Hall, John, b. 1809 or 10. New and concise method of hand-railing. V. Title.
VI. Series: Acanthus Press reprint series. 19th century, landmarks in design ; v. 2.
TT197.H235   1996
728'.092—dc20   95-50851
                                                                      CIP

Published by Acanthus Press
Barry Cenower, Publisher
54 West 21st Street
New York, NY 10010
212.463.0750
Fax 212.463.0752

Printed in the United States of America

JOHN HALL & THE GRECIAN DOMESTIC ENVIRONMENT

In 1840, an English immigrant named John Hall published three books in Baltimore dealing with household arts. *A New and Concise Method of Handrailing* introduced the "concentric ellipsograph," a machine of the author's invention which aided carpenters in laying out compound curves for stair rails and steps. *A Series of Select, Original and Modern Designs for Dwelling Houses* illustrated twenty-one designs for houses in town and country ranging from modest dwellings to one of the most palatial houses constructed in Philadelphia during the 1830s. The third title, *The Cabinet Makers' Assistant,* is Hall's only book familiar today.[1] It has frequently been cited in histories of American furniture because its images immediately convey the characteristics of the heavy and curvaceous furniture popular in 1830s and 1840s America. This genre was a development of the classical movement that dominated architectural and furniture design during the first half of the nineteenth century (fig. 1).

Today the furniture is generally called Empire and the buildings Greek Revival, but during the second quarter of the nineteenth century neither of these terms were used. Instead, the style was simply called "Grecian." John Hall frequently used this word and further characterized the version he documented as "...the present plain style of work." Both "Grecian" and "plain style" are used in this essay as descriptive terms for the furniture and architecture Hall promoted.[2]

It is remarkable that John Hall produced three books about the domestic environment in one year. On average, only four books on architectural subjects were published annually in the United States during the second quarter of the nineteenth century.[3] Shortly after Hall issued his books, a reviewer for the *Baltimore American* commented that *The Cabinet Makers' Assistant* and *Modern Designs for Dwelling Houses* had "...no connection... except that they are both by the same author, and came upon our table together."[4] It is interesting that a contemporary did not perceive that Hall's books interrelated Grecian design on two scales and this sense of aesthetic unity has also been lost on modern readers. The exceptions are Robert C. Smith, who wrote positively about Hall as early as 1958 and discussed all three of Hall's books in 1967, and Elisabeth Walton Potter, who presented Hall's designs for domestic architecture and furniture in a unified context in a 1963 study.[5] More frequently, however, *The Cabinet Makers' Assistant* has been invoked by those advocating that taste degenerated in the 1830s and 1840s.

Fifty years ago, the Americanist Carl Drepperd was the first to re-publish John Hall. Although he was ambivalent about its contents, Drepperd sponsored a reprint of *The Cabinet Makers' Assistant* because it was America's first furniture pattern book. He reinforced his negativeness by quoting an anonymous critic: "It is perhaps a pity that fate chose to motivate the portrayal of American furniture in drawing book fashion on the very eve of our era of poor furniture taste.... As one critic has remarked, 'This furniture shrieks its agony to all observers.'"[6] In 1962, Helen Comstock perpetuated disdain when she wrote that Hall's book "illustrated scrolled supports in monotonous repetition for every conceivable position."[7] Drepperd and Comstock's comments reflect the general attitude of earlier connoisseurs who favored eighteenth and early nineteenth-century American furniture. In 1965, when Charles Montgomery, the authority on Federal furniture, advised Henry Francis du Pont to purchase a flamboyant dolphin-armed sofa of about 1820 for Winterthur, he was met with the retort, "No piece of Empire was, is, or ever will be worth $2,000." The sofa was acquired by The Metropolitan Museum of Art and has been one of the prize possessions of the American Wing ever since.[8]

More recently, an exhibition called *Classical Taste in America* celebrated the pervasiveness of Grecian culture during the early nineteenth century. One of its many signs of fresh thinking is an enthusiasm for artifacts of the 1830s and 1840s. Proclaiming plain style Grecian as the culminating expression of American classical design, the catalog noted that Hall's book, "...appropriately featured the first widespread national expression in sophisticated American furniture."[9] If Drepperd's centennial re-publication of *The Cabinet Makers' Assistant* was clouded by embarrassment, this sesquicentennial reprint celebrates Hall's integrated aesthetic for domestic architecture, interiors and furniture. This reappraisal demonstrates enthusiasm for his approach to design as well as appreciation of the documentary value all three books have as indicators of taste during the antebellum period.

BIOGRAPHY

Other than his burst of publishing activity in 1840, little is known of John Hall's life and professional accomplishments. Hall was born in Devonshire in 1809 or 1810. He may have immigrated to Baltimore in the early 1830s — directories first listed him as a draftsman there in 1835 and 1837.[10] All three books designate Hall as an architect, but the Baltimore directory for 1840 lists him as a cabinetmaker. Although this trade obviously relates to Hall's best known volume, no piece of furniture has been shown to be by his hand.[11]

All three of Hall's books contain instructions on drawing methods. *The Cabinet Makers' Assistant* begins with a brief treatise on "Practical Perspective" and *Modern Designs for Dwelling Houses* ends with instructions for "Drawing Plans and Elevations." With this in mind, it is not surprising that in 1840 Hall advertised the "reopening" of a drawing school in association with "Mr. Bannan's Classical Academy."[12]

> The Drawing department is under the superintendence of Mr. JOHN HALL, who will teach Architectural, Orthographical, Isometrical, Scenographical, and Ornamental DRAWING, in the most approved and practical manner. Young Ladies, who wish to be taught Drawing, can have a separate apartment.

Hall continued to teach drawing and professional methods. As late as 1848 he wished "...to inform practical Carpenters that he is prepared to teach a system of hand railing on principles entirely new and with more accuracy than ever before discovered."[13] In 1855 Rembrandt Peale, son of the painter and inventor Charles Willson Peale, published a new edition of a drawing manual for the public schools. He showed respect for Hall's draftsmanship by incorporating three plates of furniture drawings taken from the *Cabinet Makers' Assistant*.[14]

It is not known what training John Hall had for any of his professions — architecture, carpentry, furniture design or drafting. Although parts of the prefatory text for *The Cabinet Makers' Assistant* are closely modeled on a passage by Thomas King, a prolific London publisher of furniture pattern books, this does no more than imply that Hall was trained in London. King's books were influential in the United States and Hall's access to them could have occurred on either side of the Atlantic.[15] Regarding Hall's activity in architecture, in *Modern Designs for Dwelling Houses* he states that many of the designs had been, "under the author's immediate superintendence." Unfortunately we do not know enough about how he practiced day-to-day to put this into context.

In 1846, Hall married Catherine L. Bateman in Baltimore and a daughter, Margaret, was born to the Halls the following year.[16] In 1846, a John G. Hall formed a partnership with John E. Carver, a Philadelphia builder/architect. The firm was also listed in the 1846 New York City directory. Although directories indicate that this professional relationship lasted only one or two years, Roger W. Moss's speculation that this individual was the same as the Baltimore architect is borne out by comparing a set of working drawings signed "Carver and Hall, Architects" with Hall's publication.[17] The delicately drawn pencil and watercolor construction documents depict "Stores for Thos. B. Longstreath" located at the corner of Callowhill and Second Streets in Philadelphia. The 20 foot, 6 inch frontage on Second Street is similar to Hall's elevation for a "Four Story Warehouse" illustrated on plate 20 of *Modern Designs for Dwelling Houses*. In addition, the last three bays of the lengthy Callowhill elevation follow a similar format (fig. 2). The style of dimensioning and drafting is close enough between the drawing and Hall's lithograph to confirm that he did collaborate with Carver. Why the partnership broke up is not known.

By 1847 John Hall had returned to Baltimore as an architect and the 1850 census shows that he was still practicing there at mid-century.[18] A second edition of *Dwelling Houses* was published in 1848 with an updated title page but the plates were crudely re-engraved.

VIII

Although a second edition of *The Cabinet Makers' Assistant* is said to have been issued in 1848, no copies with this date can be located.[19] By the late 1840s, plain style Grecian furniture had been superseded by the ornate rococo, Gothic and Elizabethan tastes and a second edition would not have had the relevance *Dwelling Houses* maintained.

BALTIMORE CONTEXT

An aerial view of the city of Baltimore lithographed by Edward Sachse in 1850 epitomizes the civic environment that John Hall documented on a more minute scale[20] (fig. 3). One can still glimpse fragments of similar neighborhoods built during the first half of the nineteenth century in New York, Philadelphia, Boston and Cincinnati. These retain elevations similar to the types seen in the Sachse print and all derive from eighteenth century London precedents.[21]

Hall's *Modern Designs for Dwelling Houses* can be used as a lens to focus on how the house types shown in the Sachse view were varied to suit the pocketbook of the owner. Plates 2, 4 and 6, for example, present the modest eighteen- and twenty-foot-wide configurations seen in the left-hand mid-ground of the print.[22] Sachse depicted many of the twenty-five to thirty foot sorts with three bays shown on plates 8, 10, 11 and 12. Expensive versions of these are shown in the foreground surrounding Mount Vernon Place and innumerable others are shown behind them from all angles. A variation on this type is the paired example shown in Hall's plate 24 and two such duplexes are seen on the left side of the Washington Monument. An equally large dwelling is located to the right of the monument but this is a single family house, the sumptuous five-bay Dr. J. Hanson Thomas residence of 1848.[23] This building is similar to the fifty foot wide "three story house...suitable for a large family" seen on Hall's plate 16.

No matter what the width of these dwellings, their depth ranged from forty to fifty feet. This accommodated the entry and a stair hall which flanked a pair of formal rooms on the principle floor. By not exceeding fifty feet, the front and back parlors could be both well proportioned yet shallow enough for light to penetrate from front and back windows. To accommodate service and insure adequate light and air, the back building was about ten feet narrower than the front. Hall's plans show that an even narrower "back entry" connected both buildings. In three examples the first space in the back building was a breakfast room. Others show a closet in this position and this was characteristic of row houses in Philadelphia.[24] This corner was generally curved to provide light and maneuvering and it may have had an aesthetic motivation. The kitchen, washroom and water closets were located behind the semi-public breakfast room.

The Sachse view of Baltimore and Hall's illustrations of plans, furniture and stairways come to life when related to several minutely detailed portraits of members of the Israel and Sarah Ann Griffith family. These paintings by Oliver Tarbell Eddy convey the ambiance of a prosperous 1840s American family.[25] The Griffiths' neighborhood was not clearly shown in the Sachse view, being located in the jumble of streets behind the dome and spires of Benjamin Henry Latrobe's Cathedral of the Assumption. From other documents, however, it is clear that the Griffith house followed the three bay typology so often seen in the lithograph. From what can be gathered about its architectural and interior detail, the Griffiths' taste was consistent with the aesthetic presented in all three of John Hall's books.

THE ISRAEL AND SARAH GRIFFITH HOUSEHOLD

Israel Griffith was born in 1799 and died in 1875, a Baltimore millionaire.[26] In 1824 he married his first cousin, Sarah Ann. Three years later he joined the wholesale dry goods business developed by his older brother, Henry Berry Griffith. This was located at the intersection of West Baltimore and Sharp Streets (Hopkins Place) and initially, Israel's family lived above the dry goods store. In 1832, Henry died and Israel inherited the business and took in at least one of the children, sixteen year old Jane Rebecca Griffith.

In the early 1840s the Griffiths moved into a row house built farther south on Sharp Street, one half block from Robert Mills's First Baptist Church.[27] Tax records document that the Griffiths owned two adjacent houses, one on a forty-eight foot wide lot that ran 225 feet deep from South Sharp to an alley. A smaller house was located to the north.[28] A Sanborn fire insurance map of 1879 provides the footprint of both dwellings.[29] The larger had a front building that measured twenty-eight by fifty feet in depth and its three story brick facade was capped by a wooden cornice. A "back entry" connected the front block with a back building measuring twenty feet by forty feet. A variety of wooden appendages were attached to the back and a brick stable measuring twenty-eight by twenty-five feet was situated at the rear of the lot. A narrow wooden shed spanned most of the distance between the stable and the main house and a twenty-foot-wide garden occupied the remainder of the lot to the south. Symbols on the south wall indicate that the only windows looking out to the garden were at the attic level, suggesting that the Griffiths may have anticipated construction on the open portion of the property. The side of the dwelling probably looked similar to the house next to a vacant lot to the right of Sachse's Washington Monument. The smaller two-story house built by Israel Griffith to the north had a store on the street level and a residence above. It may have both sheltered the family of Israel's deceased brother and supplied income for them.

In *Modern Designs for Dwelling Houses* nine of the twenty-one designs are row houses ranging from two to five bays in width. Hall's three-bay scheme on plate 8 can be imposed on the Griffith footprint to suggest its layout. By relating this to the details in a family portrait, the plan can be reconstructed with considerable accuracy (fig. 4). Hall's "Three story house with an attic and back building" is twenty-five feet wide but its dimensions can be easily expanded to twenty-eight. In elevation, an Ionic entry portal is located next to windows topped by cornices supported by consoles — one of the most elegant designs Hall presented. He provided an unusual amount of detail for its elements by showing an enlargement of the console and a side elevation of the porch.[30] In plan, the Ionic porch leads to a vestibule and beyond this, a narrow passage terminates in a U-shaped stair of the type detailed in plates 1-5 of *A New and Concise Method of Hand-Railing*.[31]

A large portrait of six of Israel and Sarah's ten children painted about 1844 by Oliver Tarbell Eddy depicts the drawing room and back parlor of the Griffith house[32] (fig. 5). The portrait has been reproduced frequently because it is packed with details of Grecian material culture. Given the site's configuration, the entry and passage were located to the north. Fitting this orientation to the picture, the children were gathered in the back parlor near the opening to the more formal front parlor. The pair of windows seen behind them open to a bucolic vista, but this conceit ignores the actual view. According to the Sanborn map, one would have seen a series of row houses across South Sharp Street reflecting the Griffith facade. The Sharp Street Methodist Church was located to the southwest.

A gold-framed mirror above a table rests against the brick pier between the front windows. These are partially covered by simple curtains hung from metal valances and a side chair is informally set below one window sill. In the foreground, two of the chair's mates are shown in greater detail. Israel Jr. nonchalantly sits on one while his twin, Sarah Ann, leaves hers to embrace him. These chairs are finer than Hall's "parlor chair" shown in figure 146, but both are variations on the ancient Greek *klismos* developed in France during the *Restauration*. They have cabriole front legs rather than the saber form of the *Empire*. In Hall's example, the stiles are shaped in an S-curve incorporating both back leg and crest rail support. The chairs in the Griffith painting were slightly different and were called "French chairs."[33] Because their stiles sweep forward they provide little structural support, a function carried only by the splat.

The front and back parlors in the Griffith house open to one another through sliding doors. Their frames are composed of moldings that derive from ancient Greek architecture, especially the S-shaped cyma. An expensive carpet, possibly Chenille Axminster, provides unity between the rooms with its bold pattern and characteristically vibrant colors.[34] To the far right, twelve-year-old Alverda Griffith opens the door to the passage, and from the crack we see that the floor covering changes to durable tiles. One of Hall's U-shaped stairs was probably positioned beyond this door.

Mary Eleanor, the eldest child in the picture, sits on an armchair that may be one of several "girls chairs" mentioned in the inventory of furnishings made at the death of Sarah Ann Griffith in 1877. It is covered with cut or stamped red velvet — a useful clue for upholstering plain style Grecian furniture. This chair is similar to Hall's fig. 147, "an easy chair...quite easy to sit on." Its serpentine arm supports are more convoluted than Hall's example, yet their shape is similar to the consoles of Hall's pier tables seen in figures 60-63. The scale is obviously different but, as Hall states in *The Cabinet Makers' Assistant*, "The great variety of scrolls shown in this work, with instructions for drawing them, will afford great facilities to the artisan in applying them to a great variety of work not enumerated in the present collection."[35] The skirt consists of a mitered cyma profile and this shape has already been observed in the architectural mill work. The cyma, a Greek word that means "wave", was an essential part of Grecian vocabulary, employed in endless configurations.[36] Except for the chair's bulbous front legs, all wooden surfaces are veneered with mahogany.

A portrait of the children's mother painted by Eddy about 1843 depicts additional objects owned by the family[37] (fig. 7). Sarah Ann Griffith stands in front of an upholstered easy chair that is similar to the one in the children's portrait. To her right, a marble-topped table with a cyma skirt supports a remarkable lamp. The bronze standard is embellished with rococo foliage and supports brackets for candles as well as an oil-powered unit.[38] As an example of the exuberant trappings favored for ornamenting lighting technology during the 1840s, the lamp's design is in clear contrast to the furniture's bold abstraction. By highlighting this and the unusual annular lamp that incongruously hangs just inside the drawing room door in the children's portrait, Eddy depicted pieces of metalwork that evidently had great value for the Griffiths.

About 1842, Eddy painted a small but detailed picture of Jane Rebecca Griffith[39] (fig. 6). The twenty-five year old cousin stands in a drawing room looking toward the front windows while she rests against a wildly scrolled rocking chair. Although no paintings are hung on the cream-green walls, the geometrical red, green, and black floor covering compensates for the lack of decoration. It has been assumed that this painting also documents the Griffith lodgings, but the presence of columns instead of pilasters framing the sliding doors and the simple casing around the door to the passage suggest that the room is located in a different building, possibly in the small house located to the north. The tall Corinthian columns have capitals of the unusual American type presented by Minard Lafever in *The Beauties of Modern Architecture*.[40] The columns carry a full entablature and evoke the second half of Hall's caption describing the dining room of plate 26 in *Dwelling Houses*:

> In the drawing room there are two Corinthian columns, one on each side of
> the sliding doors, supporting a projecting entablature; on the other side of
> the doors in the dining room, there are two corresponding columns, *in antae*,
> the entablature of which is not broken, but follows the line of the room.

A pair of chairs in the corner is similar to those in the children's portrait and a green baize cloth covers a center table that stands behind the subject. Like the easy chair in the other portraits, the rocking chair has a cyma-shaped skirt framing a red velvet cushion. A sofa rests against the wall between the drawing room and the passage and this voluptuous piece is also covered with red velvet upholstery. It has pillows consisting of flat pads — interesting adaptations to the square contours of the box sofa. Although cylindrical balusters are usually assumed to be appropriate for sofas of this period, they only make sense when nestled in scrolled "Grecian arms" as seen in Hall's figures 125, 126, 132, or 133. Although all of the Griffith furniture relates to the aesthetic presented in Hall's book, this sofa is identical to one Hall drew in side elevation on fig. 130 (figs. 8 & 9). Except for a few details, it also matches the perspective of fig. 140. The direct parallel between the Griffith sofa and Hall's images prompts one to wonder if Hall was employed by the Griffiths as architect or furnisher, but no documentation substantiates this idea. Nonetheless, the similarities reinforce the fact that Hall's books reflected popular taste during the 1840s.

THE DEVELOPMENT OF THE GRECIAN PLAIN STYLE

A broadside dated 1833 displays 44 images advertising furniture available at the New York "Manufactory of Cabinet and Upholstery Articles" of Joseph Meeks and Sons. Half of these pieces are plain style Grecian, including number 44 which shows a "mahogany sofa" (fig. 8) similar to the one in the portrait of Jane Rebecca Griffith (fig. 6). The scrolled feet support gigantic consoles and a haircloth cushion and back are crowned by a horizontal crest of cyma curvature. This unusually large molding was probably intended to be veneered with crotch grain mahogany set in an arcaded pattern. The date of the broadside confirms that this type of sofa was being made at least seven years before Hall's publication and a decade before its depiction in the portrait of Jane Rebecca Griffith.

The images in the Meeks circular and in Hall's *Cabinet Makers' Assistant* show continuity with earlier interpretations of the Grecian aesthetic but they also exhibit distinctly different characteristics. The typology established during the 1820s, with graceful lines, decorative carving and relatively light proportions, was reinterpreted during the 1830s with a drive toward plainness and heavier outline. The sinuous curves of sofa arms and legs, for example, once articulated with paw feet and cornucopiae, became bulky, planar forms relieved only by disk rosettes and architectural moldings. The resplendent flame patterns extracted from the crotches of mahogany trees and sawn into veneers had long been prized for application to furniture surfaces. During the 1830s, however, the glimmering patterns of this wood replaced carving as the medium for decorative expression. As the veneer was cut thinner and thinner, it could be applied to convoluted planes of tighter and tighter radius. The patterns were also adroitly positioned to emphasize the interplay of large scale furniture components.

Plain style Grecian can be viewed as the culminating expression of the classical impulse that was the primary motivation for design during the first half of the nineteenth century. The development of this phenomenon over time and on both sides of the Atlantic can be grasped by studying the evolution of a type of sideboard which was called both Grecian and Egyptian (it also had Roman elements). Despite the progressive abstraction of its forms, the underlying ideas were preserved with remarkable continuity.

EGYPTIAN SIDEBOARD

A type of ancient Roman candelabra carved from marble with three splayed facets resting on lion paws has been known from excavations since the Renaissance. The form was often employed as a base for candlesticks and in the 1770s Robert and James Adam brought this idea to Britain by publishing designs for elaborate candelabra.[41] In 1799, Charles Heathcote Tatham presented the archaeological evidence with his engravings of ancient furniture in *Etchings Representing the Best Examples of Ancient Ornamental Architecture* (fig. 9). Early nineteenth century designers extended the association with lighting devices when they used the tripod as the base for Argand-burner lamps and later technologies (fig. 10).

In 1807, Thomas Hope used the tripod as the base for a "round table" and in-so-doing freed it from its association with lighting.[42] This type of table became standard during the Regency and as late as 1825 a somewhat bulkier version was presented in *The Upholsterer's and Cabinet Maker's Pocket Assistant* by John Taylor, a Covent Garden cabinetmaker (fig. 11). Taylor published at least four books of designs for furniture and upholstery during the mid-1820s and he seems to have been responsible for a further transformation of the candelabra image.[43] An engraving in the October 1822 issue of *Ackerman's Repository of the Arts* illustrates a "sideboard and cellaret suitable for the mansions of the great and opulent"[44] (fig. 12). Rudolph Ackerman generally credited the designer of pieces featured in this segment. Although Taylor is not noted, the loose drawing style and expressive use of classical motifs strongly point to his authorship. One facet of the candelabra tripod is applied to the door of each sideboard pedestal and like the ancient source, the splayed dies bear down on clenched lion paws. At the top of each die an inverted torus molding is carved with gadrooning.[45]

About 1825 variations on the "great and opulent" sideboard began to appear in the United States (fig. 15). Despite obvious inspiration from the British source, American cabinetmakers followed local precedent by raising the whole upon stump feet. In many cases they eliminated the cellaret by filling the center with efficient storage compartments. The caption for Ackerman's plate noted, "The head (is) of elegant Grecian form...(and) should be carved of wood that has but few markings, that the workmanship may shew to advantage." The backboards of some examples from Philadelphia incorporate intricate carving but none follow the Grecian palmettes and consoles of Taylor's design. Instead they employ the vine and cornucopia motifs associated with local tradition.[46] The example shown in figure 15 has no carving at all and shows a tendency toward simplification by displaying richly patterned and symmetrically positioned crotch grain veneer. Nonetheless, it retains carved gadrooning and articulate lion paws similar to the British prototype.

A second example, possibly from Baltimore, illustrates the same form subjected to the plain style aesthetic (fig. 14). Although the overall shape replicates the earlier form line-for-line, all carved elements are replaced by planar scrolls and moldings. Another American innovation was to place a dramatic cove above each pedestal and these are actually the fronts of shallow drawers. Despite the Roman origins of the trapezoid, both recently and during the nineteenth century the combination of the tripod shape with a cove has been interpreted as Egyptian — due to its resemblance to the battered pylons of temple precincts.[47] The Egyptian association is more understandable when applying it to the later, more highly abstracted designs. In 1836, an engraving of a sideboard pedestal was published in *The Book of Prices of the United Society of Journeymen Cabinet Makers of Cincinnati* and the text described it as an "Egyptian Sideboard"[48] (fig. 13). Although the Cincinnati book is the only place where this image has survived, it is improbable that it was invented there. Because most extant sideboards were made in Philadelphia and Baltimore, it can be surmised that the image was first published in a currently lost mid-Atlantic price book of about 1832.

Price books for cabinetmakers were published in England and America from the late eighteenth through the mid-nineteenth centuries.[49] They were not pattern books like Hall's *Cabinet Makers' Assistant*. Instead, they served as contract documents that established prices cabinet shop owners should pay journeymen for executing specific tasks leading to the assembly of a whole piece of furniture. Instructions were primarily conveyed through written specifications and tables, but as time went on, engraved plates were added to depict molding profiles and components like the feet, arms and backs of sofas (fig. 16). Hall's technique of illustrating disjointed furniture components is unusual for a pattern book and it may derive from the price book convention.[50] Engravings in the price books occasionally showed how an assembled piece should appear, but this was rare. In the case of the Egyptian sideboard, however, a front and a partial side elevation of the pedestal aided the cabinetmaker's understanding of the description.

Price books document with great candor what styles were prevalent at the time of their publication. Rather than promoting a specific style, they were assembled to document the changing techniques in cabinet making brought about by demand for new designs. In the preface to the Cincinnati book, the committee stated, "...the continual change of style in cabinet work, and the introduction of new jobs; having rendered the former 1830 book almost useless, was deemed sufficient cause to bring forward the present publication." This shows that taste had changed dramatically in only six years.

The New York Book of Prices of 1834 provides useful clues about design transitions during the early 1830s.[51] It retained "old-fashioned" forms such as carved eagles and lyres perpetuated from publications of the late 1820s.[52] It also presented the bold shapes of the plain style seen in the Meeks circular of 1833. The 1836 Cincinnati book did not belie such ambivalence. Half of its patterns included plain style components copied from the 1834 New York edition and the other half, including the Egyptian sideboard, were similar designs taken from the presumably lost mid-Atlantic volume. By the mid 1830s, carved decoration was no longer in demand in Cincinnati and plain style Grecian had become dominant.

Since the design of the Egyptian sideboard was clearly available in the Queen City, a sideboard "brought down river" to Madison, Indiana, about 1840 could have been made in Cincinnati[53] (fig. 17). Whereas the general form is similar to eastern precursors, the elements are even more simplified. The vestige of the lion paws found in the scrolls supporting the trapezoid in figure 14 are eliminated. All transitions are made with moldings and the entire surface is coated with veneer to emphasize the fluidity of the rippling planes. Thick C-scrolls with applied disks substitute for the formerly turned feet. A swag embellishes the top drawer and the door below is framed like an ogee mirror. An X-shaped welt within the panel reminds one of the Philadelphia technique of applying veneer to convex, pie-shaped wedges, as practiced in the 1820s by Anthony Gabriel Quervelle and Charles H. White.[54]

Although John Hall did not illustrate the Egyptian sideboard, a similar sense of architectonic monumentality underlies all of his images. In his captions, Hall occasionally suggested that the forms he outlined were "susceptible of being highly ornamented with carvings, if taste should require it." On the other hand, they could also "be made with flat surfaces and veneered."[55] As almost all of the images he published were plain style, it seems that he was not actually promoting carving with great passion. Although the line engraving of the Egyptian sideboard could be interpreted as depicting blanks to be carved as paws and acanthus, the text emphasized that the forms should be covered with veneer. Even the scroll and "buttress" were shown dotted, a sign that they were dispensable.

The value of furniture produced in the United States during the second quarter of the nineteenth century has been debated for over a century. Appreciation has often depended on whether pieces were highly carved and gilded. The intentional lack of carving and gilding has engendered the prejudice that plain style Grecian was a decadent de-evolution of superior precedents. Simplification was a conscious move and it signaled a change from a desire to embellish objects with relief to an aesthetic in which forms were decorated with the glistening play of mahogany veneer. Great skill was required to coat compound curves and tight radii with the temperamental crotch, and price books prove that these techniques required skilled craftsmanship. As the evolution of the Egyptian sideboard shows, superficial changes did not fundamentally affect the furniture's typology — although with time, bulk did increase.

The advent of the plain style has often been explained as being a by-product of increasing dependence on steam-driven machinery and the need to cheapen materials in accommodation of middle-class economies. The price books help us evaluate whether or not the shift from carving to plain veneered surfaces was fundamentally motivated by these factors. Cost comparisons show that although they were simpler in outline, the new forms could be as expensive to produce as carved predecessors. It was costly to cut thick forms and to employ techniques of giving nuance by "sweeping" compound curves into their bulk. The price books set prices for cutting wood based on thickness. Additional width resulted in greater cost for labor and material — the bulkier the furniture, the more expensive it became. Similar factors were calculated for applying veneer. Coating curved planes with veneer was difficult and positioning grain patterns required judgment. The costs for this expert labor offset savings that might have accrued by not engaging a carver. Although some furniture in the genre was inferior in workmanship and design (flaws certainly exist in Hall's *Cabinet Makers' Assistant*, such as the tables shown in figures 156 and 157), plain style Grecian furniture should be interpreted as a change in taste, not merely a response to social or technological factors.

HALL'S RELATIONSHIP TO HIS CONTEMPORARY ARCHITECTS

The earlier discussion of architecture focused on Hall's treatment of the rowhouse. Although this urban building type provides the clearest illustration of Hall's integrated approach to architecture and interiors, *Modern Designs for Dwelling Houses* featured twice as many suburban and rural residences. Hall took a number of his designs directly from John Claudius Loudon's *Encyclopaedia of Architecture* published in 1833 in London.[56] Hall's Plate 1 varied Loudon's "Dwelling with three rooms and other conveniences." In plate 19, Hall copied aspects of Loudon's "Portable Cottage for the Use of Emigrants and Others." Hall did not refer to Loudon in either case, nor did he credit the designer of the cottage, an English carpenter named Manning who intended the structure for export to New Zealand. Hall abbreviated Loudon's text for the cottage to make the prefabricated house seem plausible for America's westward expansion — despite its impracticality for settlers who actually trudged to their destinations rather than arriving by ship. Nonetheless, an early reviewer was convinced: "...a portable cottage, for the use of new settlers, &c. This may be of service to the builders of log cabins"![57]

Hall's other designs for freestanding residences seem to derive from Regency pattern books.[58] Two exceptions are a house "...for a gentleman without any family" of plate 9 and the similarly cubic "Three Story House in the Grecian Style, adapted for a large family." Hall referred to the second as the residence of Col. John Hare Powell [sic.], Esq. and this is

ILLUSTRATIONS

1 *Pier Table*
New York or Philadelphia, ca. 1840
Mahogany, marble and mirror,
38¼ x 46 x 22½ inches

High Museum of Art, Atlanta, Georgia
Virginia Carroll Crawford Collection
1986. 191

2 CARVER AND HALL Architects
Stores for Thos. B. Longstreath
Philadelphia
Callowhill Street elevation
Pencil and watercolor wash on
J. Whatman paper, ca. 1846
(46x70cm)

The Athenaeum of Philadelphia

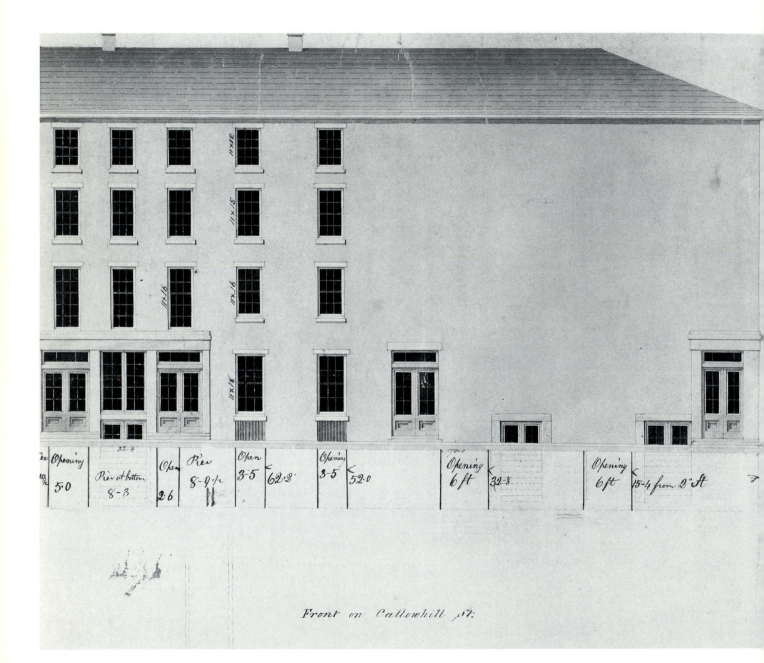

VIEW OF BALTIMORE CITY

3 EDWARD SACHSE & CO.
View of Baltimore City,
Drawn from Nature
Lithograph, 1850

The Peale Museum,
Baltimore City Life Museums
The T. Edward Hambleton Collection

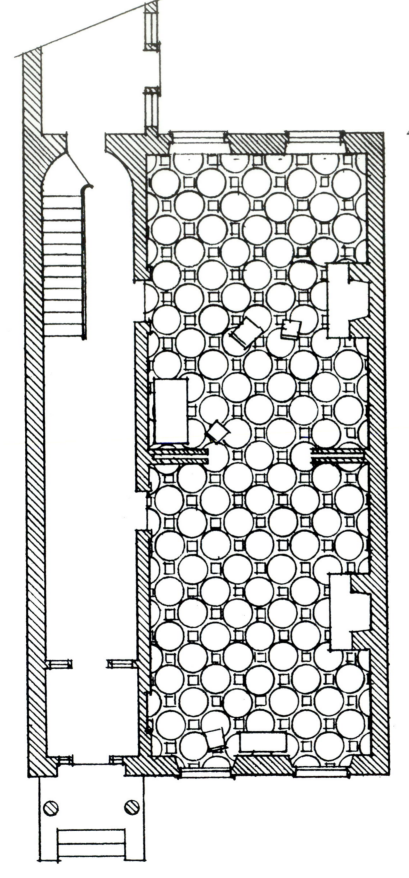

4 ISRAEL AND SARA ANN
GRIFFITH HOUSE
Conjectural plan and elevation
43 South Sharp Street,
Baltimore
built ca. 1839-40

Drawing by the author

5 OLIVER TARBELL EDDY
The Children of Israel Griffith
probably shown in the back parlor of their
Baltimore rowhouse ca. 1844
Left to right, Israel Jr. (1835-63), Sarah Ann
(1835-58), Mary Eleanor (1828-1888), Emma,
seated (1842- ?), Frances Ann (1830-63),
Alverda (1832-1901)

Maryland Historical Society, Baltimore, 18.9.1.
Gift of the Family of
Mr. and Mrs. Romulus Riggs Griffith, Jr.

6 OLIVER TARBELL EDDY (left)
Jane Rebecca Griffith
(1816-1848) ca. 1842
Oil on Wood Panel

Maryland Historical Society,
Baltimore, 36.12.1
Gift of Jane G. Keys

7 OLIVER TARBELL EDDY (right)
Mrs. Israel Griffith (Sarah Ann)
(1803-1877) ca. 1843
Oil on Canvas

Maryland Historical Society,
Baltimore, 48.73.1.
Gift of Mrs. Charles S. Robson,
Mrs. L. Farnandis Hughes,
Miss Mary Eleanor Farnandis,
Mrs. Arthur C. Montell, Jr.,
W. Walter Farnandis,
Mrs. James Hurley and
Mrs. Herbert A. Rossmann

8 ENDICOTT & SWETT
Joseph Meeks & Sons' Manufactory
of Cabinet and Upholstry Articles:
Circular No. 6 (detail).
Item no. 44, Mahogany Sofa
Watercolored Lithograph, 1833

Yale University Art Gallery,
1991.99.1 Purchased with funds
from Eleanor H. Little in memory of
May Caughey, M.Phil., 1923, by
exchange, and Everett V. Meeks,
B.A. 1901, Fund

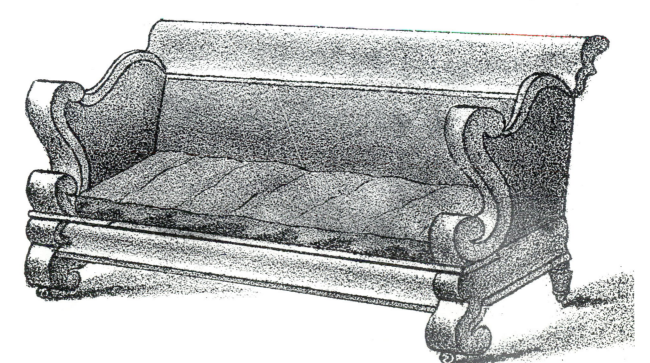

9 CHARLES HEATHCOTE TATHAM
"...An Antique (Berberini)
Candelabrum...from the Collection
in the Museum of the Vatican"

*Etchings Representing the Best
Examples of Ancient Ornamental
Architecture, 1799*

10 CORNELIUS & CO. (right)
Solar Lamp
Philadelphia, 1843

*Philadelphia
Museum of Art*
'65-211-1

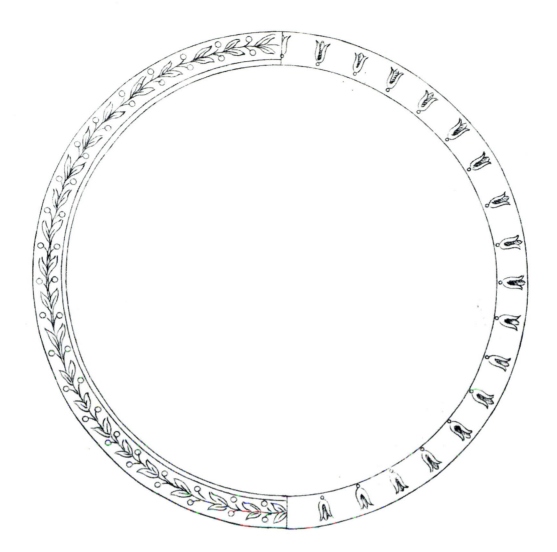

11 JOHN TAYLOR
Design for a Centre Table
from *The Upholster's and
Cabinet Makers' Pocket
Assistant,* London, 1823,
plate 24
Derived from Thomas
Hope's "round table" of
pl. XXXIX in *Household
Furniture* published in 1807

*Courtesy, The Winterthur
Library: Printed Book and
Periodical Collection*

SIDEBOARD & CELLARET.

12 JOHN TAYLOR (top)
(attributed)
Sideboard and Cellaret from
R. Ackerman's Repository of the Art,
pl. 21, p. 243, October 1822

Acanthus Books, New York

13 *Egyptian Sideboard* (below left)
Front and side elevations. Plate **14**
of the *Book of Prices of the United
Society of Journeymen of Cincinnati
for the Manufacture of Cabinet Ware,*
1836

*The Winterthur Library: Printed Book
and Periodical Collection*

14 UNKNOWN CABINET MAKER
Sideboard (below right)
Possibly Baltimore, ca. 1832
Pine with mahogany and mahogany
veneer

Didier, Inc., New Orleans

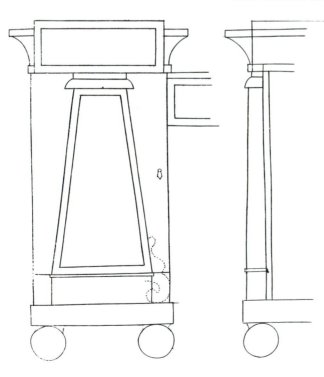

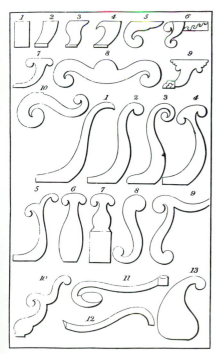

15 UNKNOWN CABINET MAKER (top)
Sideboard
Philadelphia or Baltimore, ca. 1825-30.
Mahogany and pine, 49x73½x23¾ in.

*The Art Institute of Chicago, 1974.8
Mrs. Alfred S. Burdick. Alfred T.
Carlton, Hibbard Family Heirs,
Mrs. Paul B. Magnuson, and Decorative
Arts Purchase funds*

16 *Feet and Arms for Sofas* (far left)
Unnumbered plate following plate 7
*The New York Book of Prices for
Manufacturing Cabinet and Chair
Work*, 1834

*Courtesy, The Winterthur Library:
Printed Book and Periodical Collection*

17 UNKNOWN CABINET MAKER (left)
Sideboard. Possibly Cincinnati, ca. 1836-
40. Softwood with mahogany veneer

*The Lanier State Historic Site,
Madison, Indiana*

18 DAVID JOHNSON KENNEDY
Residence built by
John Hare Powel, 1832
South west corner of Locust
and 13th, Philadelphia
Watercolor
Kennedy was in Philadelphia
between 1840 and 1870

The Historical Society of
Pennsylvania, Philadelphia
K:IV-3

19 WILLIAM STRICKLAND
(attributed)
John Hare Powel House, 1832
photograph ca. 1900
The east wing had been
renovated as a gallery and the
west wing had been replaced
by an assembly hall at the time
the photograph was taken.

The Historical Society of
Pennsylvania, Philadelphia,
Box 51, folder 1

20 Comparison of William Strickland's
attributed design for the
John Hare Powel House (right) with
John Hall's variations of 1840 (left)
Plans and north elevations

Drawing by the author

21 WILLIAM STRICKLAND (attributed)
John Hare Powel House
Philadelphia, 1832
South Elevation from the garden, ca. 1875
Photograph by F. Gutekunst

*The Historical Society of Pennsylvania,
Philadelphia, #412-453*

22 WILLIAM STRICKLAND (attributed)
John Hare Powel House 1832
Philadelphia
Interior photograph by Julius F. Sachse
looking west from the dining room
through the saloon to the drawing room,
June 24, 1889

The Historical Society of Pennsylvania,
Philadelphia, Box 51, Folder 1

23 HORACE ROCKWELL (1811-1877)
The Samuel Hanna Family, 1843
Oil on canvas, 69x63 in.

Fort Wayne Museum of Art,
Fort Wayne, Indiana
Gift of the Hanna Family Heirs, 1937.02

the only structure he identified by owner's name. The Powel house is unusual for its size and complexity and Hall lavished plates 13–15 on its illustration. He also described it in greater detail than any other structure.

THE JOHN HARE POWEL HOUSE

Construction on the Powel house began in 1832 and correspondence between John Hare Powel and William Strickland suggests that America's first great native-born architect designed the residence.[59] Although the house had its only publication in *Modern Designs for Dwelling Houses*, Hall's images are not reliable documents of its actual appearance because he made "many improvements." An early watercolor and Powel's description provide candid views of the mansion[60] (fig. 18).

> I am about to build an house 60 feet by 44 feet on Locust Street between
> 13th and Juniper Streets... I shall place myself on the frontier and although
> my friends condemn me for leaving what is termed the fashionable part of
> town I am satisfied in having two hundred feet at the cost of 40 near the
> house of [his aunt and adoptive mother] Mrs. Powel.

By the turn of the twentieth century, the Col. John Hare Powel House was no longer in the "frontier" and a photograph shows that the central block was the only portion to retain its original configuration (fig. 19). Greek Doric columns supported a spare entablature and this portico was the most articulate element of the façade. The cornice terminated below a string course dividing the facade into two registers — the upper punctuated with bedroom and sitting area windows. Above these, attic windows were compressed under an entablature. The oblique view of the photograph shows that the entablature and regular window spacing existed only on the street facade because the side windows were irregularly placed in response to functional disposition.

When the photograph is compared to the elevation in *Modern Designs for Dwelling Houses*, we see that Hall radically altered Strickland's concept (fig. 20). Most dramatically, Strickland designed the facade with four window bays rather than Hall's three — Hall seems to have been compelled to place a window on axis. Hall must also have disliked the severity of Strickland's design because he embellished the punched window openings with casings. Hall also enlarged the scale of the entablature that capped the facade by employing the same type Strickland had chosen for the Doric portico. The proportional symmetries of this entablature derived from the Choragic Monument of Thrasyllus, built in Athens in 319 BC — one of the monuments meticulously documented in the second volume of *The Antiquities of Athens* by Stuart & Revett.[61] The proportions of the Choragic Monument, like many of the Athenian buildings detailed in their engravings, were canonized by compilers of nineteenth century British and American pattern books and served as paradigms for the new Grecian structures. Strickland's taste for what could be called plain style Grecian had left the corners unarticulated but Hall transformed the entablature into a trabeated element by applying antae above the quoins.

A photograph of the garden side of the Powel house shows that Strickland's design for the rear elevation was even more severe than the front (fig. 21). One innovation was to place a window directly above the central fireplace and Hall emphasized this feature in the text and showed it in plan and elevation. Otherwise, Hall changed most aspects of the actual design in his plate 15. The photograph shows that the bay windows projecting from the drawing and dining rooms terminated below a broad Doric porch with wide intercolumniations. Hall omitted the full-length portico and positioned an Ionic porch on axis instead. He extended the bay windows vertically to the cornice, providing greater modulation to what was actually a severe facade. Finally, Hall terminated the entablature above antae on the back corners, implying that the trabeation on the front extended around the sides.

Hall introduced *Modern Designs for Dwelling Houses* with the prefatory comment: "Most of those designs have been selected from the best examples of dwellings already finished; many of them during their erection, being under the author's immediate superintendence. This experience has enabled him to make many improvements, which he conceives will render them more acceptable." Considering that Hall made audacious changes to a major residence by one of America's premier Grecian architects, how can this statement be interpreted? Did Hall work in a supervisory capacity on the Powel house upon his arrival in the United States? Or is this merely an example of a variation on a master's theme by an otherwise obscure young architect?

Drawings that document the plan of the John Hare Powel house are preserved in a set of ink-on-linen working drawings made in 1905 by Addison Hutton. These were the first stage of a project to build the current headquarters of The Historical Society of Pennsylvania. They show that portions of the Powel house were intended to be maintained as a structural armature for the re-configured building.[62] They document that the central three-story portion of the Powel house measured sixty feet in width by forty-four feet in depth. A pair of sixteen foot wide, one and a half story wings were nearly as deep as the central structure. Photographs of the interior of the John Hare Powel house show that Hall's disposition of rooms was generally true to Strickland's scheme[63] (fig. 22). Mrs. Lindsay Patterson's description of the house from childhood memories adds something of its character.

The interior was curiously arranged with huge bedrooms out of all proportion to the rest of the house, and an inexplicable squandering of space for the tripartite stairway in the center of the building, though I believe that was considered very imposing with its wrought iron balusters and mahogany rails inlaid with ivory. From the front door was entered a dimly lighted entresol, from which opened five doors.

The first door to the right of the entresol led into a small reception room.... The main door opened into the stairway hall, and that again into three rooms — the dining room, the reception room [saloon], which opened on the spacious back porch, and the drawing room, opening into the conservatory and also into the small reception room.... Folding doors enabled these rooms to be thrown into one in times of big entertainments.

Shortly after its completion, the Powel dwelling was sold. *A Catalogue of the Household Furniture... to be Sold at Public Sale* of 1836 notes that imported and domestic furnishings, accessories, books and wines were auctioned.[64] Most of the items had never been used, indicating that although Powel anticipated moving into the house in 1832, he probably did not occupy it. The catalogue provides a room-by-room account and helps us visualize the sumptuous furniture, lighting devices, carpets and accessories required to outfit a fine dwelling. Given John Hall's simultaneous interest in domestic architecture and furniture, it should be emphasized that the Powel House and the items auctioned represent a higher standard than that which was illustrated in *The Cabinet Makers' Assistant*. Dwellings for upper middle class families like the Griffiths were refined, yet their luxury did not approach that of the John Hare Powel house.

DISSEMINATION OF THE PLAIN STYLE

Cabinetmakers in Philadelphia, Baltimore and other eastern centers manufactured vast quantities of furniture in the 1830s and 1840s. With improved transportation, they were able to ship their products across the United States and this probably had more impact on the spread of the plain style Grecian than the publication of price books or John Hall's volumes.[65] We have seen that plain style Grecian design was standard in Cincinnati in 1836. Truly refined houses were being built around 1840 along the Ohio River and some of them show traces of influence from the publications of John Hall and Minard Lafever.[66] One of the most impressive is the James F.D. Lanier house completed in 1844 by Francis Costigan in Madison, Indiana. Recent success in reacquiring original furniture for the house shows that the principle rooms were furnished with plain style Grecian pieces. At the same time, plain style Grecian furniture was also available in more remote places. An 1843 portrait by Horace Rockwell of the Samuel Hanna family of Fort Wayne, Indiana, depicts a genre familiar from the portraits by Oliver Tarbell Eddy[67] (fig. 23). The Hanna family is gathered around a center table supported by three thick S-scrolls. These rest on a triangular plinth embellished with a welted star having points oriented toward each console. All of these plain style elements are simplifications of elaborate center tables made about 1830 by Anthony Quervelle.[68] The Hanna table could have been imported from the mid-Atlantic or from Cincinnati, but it also could have been made in Fort Wayne. The round top is ornamented with crotch veneer applied in pie-shaped wedges similar to Hall's figure 187 and, if made in Indiana, these flitches may have been the more readily available walnut which could be stained in imitation of mahogany.

In conclusion, we should not think of these provincial strains of plain style Grecian as being its last expression. During the last years of Duncan Phyfe's career, his shop produced elegant variations on the plain style theme. Beyond this, the American plain style in architecture and furniture is an important component of an international Grecian movement of the 1830s and 1840s. The American genre was at times even more extreme than the similarly severe, classical, *Biedermeier* furniture of the German-speaking world.[69] Chronologically, John Hall stands at the center of the movement. He at once provided a chronicle of fifteen years of development by architects and cabinetmakers/designers and his books stimulated the spread and development of the plain style approach until the Civil War.

THOMAS GORDON SMITH   †JUNE, 1995

The research for this essay was primarily conducted in the summer of 1994 on a Winterthur Research Fellowship. Neville Thompson and Donald Fennimore provided invaluable assistance. In addition, Robert L. Alexander, Jeffrey A. Cohen, Stephen Falatko, Helen W. Griffith, Eileen Gordon, Paul Goudy, Ike Hay, Roger Moss, Elizabeth Walton Potter, Page Talbott, Catherine Hoover Voorsanger and Gail Caskey Winkler have been extremely generous with ideas. The staff at The Athenaeum of Philadelphia, The Maryland Historical Society, The Peale Museum of the Baltimore City Life Museums and The Pennsylvania Historical Society have also been very helpful with material from their collections. I would like to thank the publisher, Barry Cenower, for sponsoring this project.

NOTES

1. According to citations on the title pages, the order of issue was: 1) *The Cabinet Makers' Assistant* 2) *Modern Designs for Dwelling Houses* 3) *Method of Handrailing*. From the preface of "Dwelling Houses" we know that the book was issued in four monthly installments, a common practice of the time.

2. John Hall, *The Cabinet Makers' Assistant*, Caption for plate XII, Figures 64-68, p.25 reads, "The whole of these scrolls are adapted to the present plain style of work." Over the years a number of terms have been concocted to describe the type of furniture John Hall presented. Currently popular are *Late Classical* and *Late Empire*. The most inappropriate, *Pillar and Scroll*, seems to have been coined by the sympathetic Celia Jackson Otto in the early 1960s. Although this term is descriptive of the architectural and fluid qualities of the furniture, it is irrelevant to nineteenth-century terminology and should be abandoned. The re-introduction of *Grecian*, a term employed throughout the early nineteenth century in both England and America, and the descriptive *plain style* revive period terminology and can be applied to both furniture and architecture.

3. Henry-Russell Hitchcock, *American Architectural Books*. Minneapolis: University of Minnesota Press, 1946, 1962. In his list of architectural books published in the United States before 1895, Hitchcock did not cite stair manuals or books on furniture. According to a "chronological short-title list" compiled under the direction of William H. Jordy and published as an appendix in the 1976 Da Capo reprint, during the 1830s and 1840s the number of architectural books published each year averaged four. After 1847, the number doubled.

4. From a review of *The Cabinet Makers' Assistant* and *Modern Designs for Dwelling Houses* published in *The Baltimore American* prior to 1848. This quote was reprinted along with two other reviews as an advertisement bound with the 1848 edition of *Dwelling Houses* owned by The Maryland Historical Society.

5. Robert C. Smith, "Late Classical Furniture in the United States, 1820-1850." *Antiques*, LXXIV, (December 1958): 519-523.
Elisabeth Walton (Potter), "The Baltimore Career of John Hall, Architect." A research paper for Frank Sommer for a course at Winterthur Museum through the University of Delaware, 1963. On file at the DAPC Archive, Henry Francis du Pont Winterthur Museum.
Robert C. Smith, "John Hall, A Busy Man in Baltimore." *Antiques*, XCII (September 1967): 360-366.

6. Carl Drepperd, "A note of comment on this reprint." *The Cabinet Makers' Assistant by John Hall*. New York: National Superior, 1944.

7. Helen Comstock, *American Furniture; Seventeenth, Eighteenth and Nineteenth Century Styles*. New York: Bonanza Books, 1962, 27.

8. Donald Fennimore is the source for the story. The dolphin sofa is reproduced in: Marshall B. Davidson and Elizabeth Stillinger, *The American Wing at The Metropolitan Museum of Art*. New York: Alfred A. Knopf, 1985, 158-159. In correspondence with the author, Roger W. Moss states that during the mid-1960s Charles Montgomery had students at Winterthur read and discuss, *Classical America, 1815-1845*, the catalog for a 1963 exhibition at the Newark Museum organized by Berry B. Tracy. Moss feels that Francis James Dallet and Robert C. Smith were among the first to assemble a public collection of "Empire" objects to furnish the ground floor of the Athenaeum of Philadelphia. These were also the years when Mrs. John F. Kennedy was soliciting donations of classical furniture for several rooms in the White House.

9. Wendy A. Cooper, *Classical Taste in America, 1800-1840*. New York: Abbeville Press, 1993, 214.

10. *Matchett's Baltimore Director for 1835 '36*. "John Hall, draftsman, Park btwn Saratoga & Mulberry."
Matchett's Baltimore Director for 1837 '38, "John Hall, draftsman, 148 Liberty."
Matchett's Baltimore Director for 1840 '41. "John Hall, cabinet maker, 37 1/2 N. Howard St."

11. Robert C. Smith, "John Hall, a Busy Man in Baltimore." *Antiques*, XCII (September 1967):361. Smith provided no documentation other than "family tradition" to substantiate the claim that the chest of drawers in figure 2 was made in John Hall's cabinet shop.

12. "Drawing School." *The Baltimore Sun*, VII, (October 14, 1840): 2. Reference from Elisabeth Walton (Potter). "The Baltimore Career of John Hall, Architect," Appendix L.
Jeffrey A. Cohen, "Building a Discipline: Early Institutional Settings for Architectural Education in Philadelphia, 1804-1890." *Journal of the Society of Architectural Historians*, Vol. 53, No. 2 (June 1994). This article provides a parallel for John Hall's teaching.

13. "Useful Knowledge for Mechanics," printed on an advertisement sheet inserted as the first page of the 1848 copy of *Modern Designs for Dwelling Houses* owned by The Maryland Historical Society.

14. Rembrandt Peale, *Graphics, the Art of Accurate Delineation; a System of School Exercises, for the Education of the Eye and the Training of the Hand...*Philadelphia: E.C. & J. Biddle. Plates XIV, XV, XVI.

Carol Eaton Heyner. *Rembrandt Peale, 1778-1860, A Life in the Arts*. Philadelphia: The Historical Society of Pennsylvania, 1985. 13, 16.

15. Thomas King, *The Modern Style of Cabinet Work Exemplified*. London: T. King, 1829. Reprint, New York: Dover Publications, Inc., 1995. Between 1823 and 1842, King published twenty-six titles on furniture design, upholstery and architecture. In 1833, London directories designated King as a "publisher of designs for household furniture." *The Modern Style of Cabinet Work Exemplified* was King's most influential book, going through many editions between 1829 and 1862. Hall clearly had access to this book because he mined King's introductory "Address" to write his "Preface" for *The Cabinet Maker's Assistant* (see introduction to the Dover reprint). In addition, Hall employed the same horizontal format for *The Cabinet Makers' Assistant* as King had used for *Original Designs for Cabinet Furniture*. Hall could have easily become familiar with his countryman's books once in the United States. A leaflet of the New York bookseller, Joseph Stanley & Co., in the Winterthur library lists seven of King's titles available in 1836.

16. The Dielman–Hayward card file at The Maryland Historical Society quotes a notice from *The Easton Star* of 27 October 1846, "Married in Baltimore by Rev. Mr. Peck at the Church of the Ascension, John Hall, of Devonshire." Between 1838 and 1848 The Rev. Francis Peck was rector of the Episcopal mission church located on Lexington Street east of Pine in Baltimore.

17. Sandra L. Tatman and Roger W. Moss, *Biographical Dictionary of Philadelphia Architects, 1700-1930*. Boston: G.K. Hall, 1985, p. 331. Roger W. Moss informed me of the drawings. The ninth edition of *McElroy's Philadelphia Directory for 1846* listed Carver and Hall, architects, at 51 N. 6th St. The firm of Carver and Hall also appears in the 1846 New York City directory at 31 Wall Street.

18. *Matchett's Baltimore Director for 1847'48*. "John Hall, Architect, 19 Exchange Building."
The 1860 census for Philadelphia lists a John G. Hall as a gentleman from England with an estate of $10,000 living at the Continental Hotel. Other than having the same middle initial, nothing confirms that this is the same individual and a four year discrepancy in age does not support a parallel.

19. The 1972 edition of *The National Union Catalogue* lists three libraries which hold copies of an 1842 second edition of *The Cabinet Makers' Assistant*. None of these copies exists at present, suggesting that the entry is mistaken.

20. Lois B. McCauley, *Maryland Historical Prints, 1752-1889*. Baltimore: Maryland Historical Society, 1975. 12-13.

21. Dan Cruickshank and Neil Burton, *Life in the Georgian City*. New York: Viking Penguin Inc., 1990.

22. Mary Ellen Hayward, "Urban Vernacular Architecture in Nineteenth-Century Baltimore." *Winterthur Portfolio*. Vol. 16, No. 1 (Spring 1981): 33-63. Natalie W. Shivers, *Those Old Placid Rows, the Aesthetic and Development of the Baltimore Rowhouse*. Baltimore: Maclay and Associates, Inc., 1981.

23. Katharine B. Dehler, *The Thomas-Jencks-Gladding House*. Baltimore: Bodine & Associates, Inc., 1968. 7-25.

24. Jeffrey A. Cohen made this observation in relation to Philadelphia fire insurance surveys.

25. Edith Bishop, *Oliver Tarbell Eddy, 1799-1868*. Newark: The Newark Museum, 1950.

26. "Death of a Retired Merchant," *The Baltimore Sun*. January 20, 1875, 4. From the Dielman–Hayward File at The Maryland Historical Society.

27. Rhodri Windsor Liscombe, *Altogether American, Robert Mills, Architect and Engineer*. New York: Oxford University Press, 1994, 74.

28. Baltimore city directories listed the Griffith residence as 45 South Sharp Street from 1845 to 1853-54. After 1855, the residence was listed at 43 South Sharp until 1874. The Baltimore City Archives has tax records of 1846 for the two properties in RG4 S2. Thanks to Robert L. Alexander, Eileen Gordon and Helen W. Griffith for their help on the Griffith properties.

29. *Baltimore, Maryland*. New York: The Sanborn Map and Publishing Company, 1879, Vol. 1, map 2. Collection: The Peale Museum, The Baltimore City Life Museums.

30. During the 1830s Asher Benjamin, the prolific compiler of architectural pattern books, published two popular volumes presenting Grecian details and methods. These books are completely different from Hall's *Dwelling Houses* because Benjamin presented few whole buildings, and those were churches. Benjamin's books contained large scale engravings of Grecian architectural details and instructions for executing them. In this case, the builder would assemble parts to compose a whole rather than having the overall format available with little or no instruction on detail. One wonders if Hall assumed that the builder would rely on other resources such as Benjamin or Minard Lafever when following his instructions for a whole building. See: Asher Benjamin. *Practice of Architecture* and *The Builder's Guide*. New York: Da Capo Press, 1994.

31. The more expansive "elliptic" stair shown on plate 6 of *Method of Handrailing* could not fit within the Griffiths' twenty-eight foot plot. Hall employed it in the thirty-five foot wide "three story house with a back building" on plates 11 and 12. It is interesting to see how additional width allowed for this extraordinary stair. This demonstrates how standard configurations found in the narrower types could be maintained while adjacent variations were accommodated.

32. Emma, the child playing on the floor, was born October 1842. If she was twelve to eighteen months old, the picture would have been completed about 1844.

33. The United Society of Journeymen Cabinet Makers of Cincinnati, *Book of Prices for the Manufacture of Cabinet Ware*. Cincinnati: 1836, 90-91 and plate 12, fig. 4.

34. Gail Caskey Winkler suggested this as the type of carpet due to the variety of colors. The painting also shows that the surface had the texture of small loops.

35. John Hall's preface to *The Cabinet Makers' Assistant*.

36. In the caption for plate VI of *The Cabinet Makers' Assistant*, Hall describes figure 25 as a "Grecian ogee or cyma recta."

37. Stella Blum, *Fashions and Costumes from Godey's Lady's Book*. New York: Dover Publications, Inc., 1985, 12. Similarity to dress "b" of May, 1843, suggests a date for the portrait.

38. This lamp is similar to an earlier example at Winterthur which combines an Argand-burner fixture with brackets for candles.

39. Stella Blum, *Fashions and Costumes from Godey's Lady's Book*. New York: Dover Publications, Inc., 1985, 11. Similarity to dress "c" of October, 1842, suggests a date for this portrait.

40. Minard Lefever, *The Beauties of Modern Architecture*. New York: D. Appleton & Co., 1833, plate 11. Reprint: New York: Da Capo Press, 1968.

41. Elizabeth White, *Pictorial Dictionary of British 18th Century Furniture Design*. Woodbridge, Suffolk: The Antique Collectors' Club Ltd., 1990, 307.

42. Thomas Hope, *Household Furniture and Interior Decoration*. London: Longman, Hurst, Rees and Orme, 1807, plate XXXIX. Reprinted as *Regency Furniture and Interior Decoration*. New York: Dover Publications, Inc., 1971.

43. John Taylor, *Upholster's Magazine for 1823*. London: J. Taylor, at his Repository, 1823. Eighteen plates. (National Art Library, Victoria and Albert Museum).

John Taylor, *The Upholsterer's and Cabinet Maker's Pocket Assistant, Being a Collection of Designs for Fashionable Upholstery and Cabinet Work*. London: J. Taylor, Architectural Library, 1825-26. Two volumes with fifty plates each. (National Art Library, Victoria and Albert Museum)

John Taylor, *Taylor's Modern Upholstery*. London: Messrs Ackerman, c1825. Eighteen plates. (Avery Library of Columbia University. Peabody Library, Baltimore)

John Taylor, "Designs for Beds" (no title page). London c1827-29. (National Art Library, Victoria and Albert Museum)

44. *Ackerman's Repository of the Arts*, October 1822, plate 21, p. 243.

45. The evolution of the sideboard from a table to an elaborate case piece requires further study. The appliqué of the candelabra facet recalls a mid-stage of development illustrated by George Smith in plates 92 and 93 of his *Collection of Designs for Household Furniture* issued between 1804 and 1808. As Sheraton also shows in plate 32 of the *Encyclopaedia* of 1804, Smith shows free standing pedestals that support Greek and Egyptian figures. These flank a sideboard table. One American example of the candelabra tripod type is a pair of free-standing units in the Castle Collection of The Smithsonian Institution.

46. The resemblance of the sideboard pedestal to the candelabra tripod type was noted by Milo M. Naeve, *The Classical Presence in American Art*. Chicago: The Art Institute of Chicago, 1978, 22. Ten examples of the sideboard are known to exist and more will undoubtedly surface. Two of the highly carved examples are illustrated.

Oscar P. Fitzgerald, *Three Centuries of American Furniture*. New York: Gramercy Publishing Company, 1985, 124. Luke Vincent Lockwood, *Colonial Furniture in America*. New York: Charles Scribner's Sons, 1951, 207.

47. Donald Fennimore, "Egyptian Influence in Early Nineteenth-Century American Furniture." *The Magazine Antiques*, CXXXVII (May 1990): 1190-1201. Terminology becomes confusing: how can the term Grecian be applied to a piece in which a Roman allusion is ultimately called Egyptian? In the 1830s, people seem to have had few problems with such ambiguities because the design sensibility was syncretic and motifs were intermingled. As all of the paradigms were considered ancient, they were in sharp contrast to the concurrent alternatives of Elizabethan, Gothic or the revival of the French rococo types, broadly labeled "Old French" and "Louis Quatorze."

48. United Society of Journeymen Cabinet Makers of Cincinnati, *Book of Prices...for the Manufacture of Cabinet Ware*. Cincinnati: 1836, 34-35, Plate 14. (Winterthur Library, Printed Book and Periodical Collection.)

49. Charles F. Montgomery, *American Furniture, The Federal Period*. New York: Viking Press, 1966, 19-26, 488-89.

50. In 1829 Thomas King showed alternate components for furniture in *The Modern Style of Cabinet Work Exemplified*. Although these depicted the whole end of a sofa, for example, including the feet and complete arms, Hall treated his elements in a kit-of-parts manner.

51. Society of Journeymen Cabinet Makers, *The New York Book of Prices for Manufacturing Cabinet and Chair Work*. New York: Harper & Brothers, 1834. (Winterthur Museum, Printed Book and Periodicals Collection)

52. Cabinet and Chair Makers', *Philadelphia ...Union Book of Prices for Manufacturing Cabinet Ware*. Philadelphia: 1828. The identical plates were issued in: Cincinnati Cabinet Makers, *Book of Prices, for Manufacturing Cabinet Ware*. Cincinnati: Whetstone and Buxton, 1830. (The New-York Historical Society) and again in: Cabinet Makers, *The Pittsburgh ...Book of Prices*. Pittsburgh: Joseph Snowden, 1830. (Winterthur Museum, Printed Book and Periodicals Collection)

53. Tradition of the descendants of Dr. James Tilton, who brought the sideboard "down river" to Madison, Indiana, where he lived in the early 1840s.

54. Hall illustrated this technique with a type of radiating pattern in his pedestal sideboard of fig. 187.

55. John Hall, *The Cabinet Makers' Assistant*. Captions for plates XXII and XLIII.

56. John Claudius Loudon, *An Encyclopaedia of Cottage, Farm, and Villa Architecture and Furniture*. London: Longman, Rees, Orme, Brown, Green, & Longman, 1833. Plate LXV, p. 205 and numbers 445-457, pp. 251-257.

57. From a review of *Modern Designs for Dwelling Houses* published in *The Baltimore American* prior to 1848. This quote was reprinted as part of an advertisement bound with the 1848 edition of *Dwelling Houses* owned by The Maryland Historical Society.

58. Hall's design on Plate III may be a variation on the "Single Cottage" illustrated in: E.W. Trendall, *Original Designs for Cottages and Villas*. London: 1831, plates I-V.

59. A letter from William Strickland to John Hare Powel at the State Senate in Harrisburg, Pennsylvania, of January 11, 1830 provides advice for a railroad bridge over the Schuylkill River near Fairmount in Philadelphia. Prior to construction of the house, Powel and Strickland were clearly in professional contact. (The Historical Society of Pennsylvania, Powel Collection, 1582)

60. B. Keven Hawkins, "Historical Survey of the Property on the Southwest Corner of Locust and Thirteenth Streets: Once the Site of the Mansion of John Hare Powel." Paper for Roger W. Moss's course at the University of Pennsylvania, December 1985. (Collection: The Athenaeum of Philadelphia)

61. James Stuart and Nicholas Revett, *The Antiquities of Athens, Vol. II*. London: John Nichols 1787. Plates III & IV. Reprint: New York: Benjamin Blom, 1968.

62. I am grateful to Jeffrey A. Cohen for pointing out the blueprints for the construction of The Historical Society of Pennsylvania headquarters. The linen tracings are in the collection of the Athenaeum of Philadelphia.

63. Mrs. Lindsay Patterson, "The Old Patterson Mansion, The Master and His Guests." *Pennsylvania Magazine of History and Biography*, XXXIX, (June 1915), 83.

64. C.J. Wolbert. *Catalogue of the Household Furniture part of the Books, Plate, Wines & c. of Col J. Hare Powel to be sold at Public Sale ... on Tuesday, 19th April, 1836*. This remarkable document was found by B. Keven Hawkins in the Powel papers of the Pennsylvania Historical Society, Box 17, Folder 4.

65. The 1848 edition of *A Series of Select and Modern Designs for Dwelling Houses* was published in Pittsburgh as well as Baltimore and Philadelphia.

66. In addition to the James F.D. Lanier house, the Shrewsbury house of 1848 also built in Madison, Indiana, by the native Baltimore builder/architect, Francis Costigan, was heavily influenced by Minard Lafevers' *Beauties of Modern Architecture*. Its spectacular free-standing spiral stair, however, bears traces of Hall's *Method of Handrailing*. See: Roger G. Kennedy, *Greek Revival America*. New York: Stewart, Tabori and Chang, 1989, figs 308, 309.

67. Dean A. Porter and Robert A. Yassin, *Images of Memory: 200 Years of Indiana Art*. South Bend: University of Notre Dame, 1977, 34, 58.

68. Wendy A. Cooper, *Classical Taste in America: 1800-1840*. New York: Abbeville Press, 1993, 60-61.

69. Charles L. Venable, "Philadelphia Biedermeier: Germanic Craftsmen and Design in Philadelphia 1820-1850." Thesis for the University of Delaware, 1986. Images from many German pattern books are reproduced in the titles on Beidermeier furniture by Georg Himmelheber. They generally depict whole pieces of furniture, not parts. An interesting parallel to John Hall's book is the reprint of: Karl Matthän, *Neustes Lehr-Modell- und Ornamentenbuch für Ebenisten...*Weimar: Bernhard Friedrich Boigt, 1840. Reprint, Hannover: Th. Schäfer Druckerei, 1983.

BIBLIOGRAPHY

Bishop, Robert. *The American Chair, Three Centuries of Style*. New York: E.P. Dutton, 1972.

Bishop, Robert. *Guide to American Antique Furniture*. New York: Galahad Books, 1973.

Bishop, Robert and Particia Coblentz. *The World of Antiques, Art and Architecture in Victorian America*. New York: E.P. Dutton, 1979.

Bowman, John S. *American Furniture*. Greenwich: Brompton Books, 1985.

Butler, Joseph T. *American Antiques, 1800-1900, A Collector's History and Guide*. New York: The Odyssey Press, 1965.

Comstock, Helen. *American Furniture, Seventeenth, Eighteenth and Nineteenth Century Styles*. New York: Bonanza Books, 1962.

Cooper, Wendy A. *Classical Taste in America, 1800-1840*. New York: Abbeville Press, 1993.

Davidson, Marshall B. *The American Heritage History of American Antiques from the Revolution to the Civil War*. New York: American Heritage Publishing Co., 1969.

Downs, Joseph. *The Greek Revival in the United States, A Special Loan Exhibition*. New York: The Metropolitan Museum of Art, 1943.

Drepperd, Carl W. A Note of Comment on this Reprint *The Cabinet Makers Assistant Designed, Drawn and Published by John Hall, Architect*. New York: National Superior Inc, 1944.

Drepperd, Carl W. *Pioneer America; Its First Three Centuries*. Garden City: Doubleday & Company 1949.

Elder, William Voss, III. *Baltimore Painted Furniture 1800-1840*. Baltimore: Baltimore Museum of Art, 1972.

Fairbanks, Johnathan L. and Elizabeth Bidwell Bates. *American Furniture, 1620 to the Present* . New York: Richard Marek, 1981.

Fitzgerald, Oscar P. *Three Centuries of American Furniture*. New York: Gramercy Publishing Company, 1982.

Gowans, Alan. *Images of American Living*. Philadelphia: J.B. Lippencott, 1964.

Hayward, Mary Ellen. "Urban Vernacular Architecture in Nineteenth-Century Baltimore." *Winterthur Portfolio*. Vol. 16, No. 1, Spring 1981, 33-63.

Joy, Edward T. "The Overseas Trade in Furniture in the Nineteenth Century". *Furniture History*, Vol. VI, 1970, 69.

Miller, Edgar G., Jr. *American Antique Furniture, A Book for Amateurs*. New York: M. Barrows & Co., 1937.

Naeve, Milo M. *Identifying American Furniture*. Nashville: The American Association for State and Local History, n.d.

Otto, Celia Jackson. *American Furniture of the Nineteenth Century*. New York: The Viking Press, 1965.

Otto, Celia Jackson. "Pillar and Scroll: Greek revival furniture of the 1830s." *Antiques*. (May 1962): 31, 5, 506-507.

Poesch, Jessie. *The Art of the Old South*. 1560-1860. New York: Harrison House, 1989.

Schwartz, Marvin D. "Victorian Furniture." *The Concise Encyclopedia of American Antiques*. New York: Hawthorn Books, n.d...

Ramirez, Jan Seidler. "The Re-Dressing of a Boston Empire Sofa."*Upholstery in America & Europe from the Seventeenth Century to World War I*. New York: W.W. Norton & Co., 1987, 222, 223 (fig. 224).

Shivers, Natalie W. *Those Old Placid Rows, the Aesthetic and Development of the Baltimore Rowhouse*. Baltimore: Maclay and Associates, Inc., 1981.

Smith, Robert C. "John Hall, a Busy Man in Baltimore." *Antiques*. XCII (September 1967): 360-366.

Smith, Robert C. "Late Classical Furniture in the United States, 1820-1850."*Antiques*. LXXIX, No. 6 (December 1958): 519-523.

Tracy, Berry B. *19th Century America, Furniture and Other Decorative Arts*. New York: The Metropolitan Museum of Art, 1970.

Tracy, Berry B. *Classical America, 1815-1845*. Newark: The Newark Museum Association, 1963.

Walton (Potter), Elizabeth. "The Baltimore Career of John Hall, Architect" Research paper at Winterthur for a course at the University of Delaware. May 1964. Filed in the DAPC Archive, Winterthur Museum.

Weidman, Gregory R. and Jennifer F. Goldsborough. *Classical Maryland, 1815-1845*. Baltimore: Maryland Historical Society, 1993.

Weidman, Gregory R. *Furniture in Maryland, 1740-1940*. Baltimore: Maryland Historical Society, 1984.

Yates, Raymond F. and Marquerite W. *A Guide to Victorian Antiques*. New York: Grosset & Dunlap, 1949.

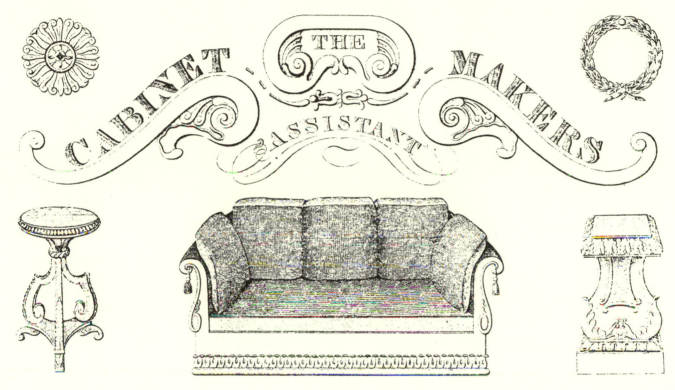

THE
CABINET MAKERS
ASSISTANT

Lith. by E. Weber & Co

DESIGNED, DRAWN AND PUBLISHED, BY JOHN HALL,
ARCHITECT,
BALTIMORE

THE
CABINET MAKERS' ASSISTANT,

EMBRACING THE

MOST MODERN STYLE OF CABINET FURNITURE:

Exemplified in New Designs, practically arranged on forty-four Plates containing one hundred and ninety-eight Figures:

TO WHICH IS PREFIXED

A SHORT TREATISE

ON

LINEAR PERSPECTIVE,

FOR THE USE OF PRACTICAL MEN.

By JOHN HALL, ARCHITECT AND DRAFTSMAN.

BALTIMORE:
PRINTED BY JOHN MURPHY, 146 MARKET STREET.
::::::::::::::::::
1840.

PREFACE.

NOVELTY, simplicity and practicability, are blended with the present designs, in which originality mostly prevails; a few of those designs have been taken from work previously executed, in consequence of their being highly approved. As far as possible, the style of the United States is blended with European taste, and a graceful outline and simplicity of parts are depicted in all the objects. The present work will not only be useful to the manufacturer, but of great importance to persons who may order furniture, as they will be enabled to select their patterns and have them executed without any misunderstanding. The great variety of scrolls shown in this work, with instructions for drawing them, will afford great facilities to the artizan in applying them to a great variety of work not enumerated in the present collection. The short treatise on perspective will be found of the utmost importance to

every cabinet-maker, as they can acquire, by a very little study of those principles, a sufficient knowledge to enable them to draw with accuracy any piece of work that may present itself to their mind. Throughout the whole of the designs in this work, particular attention has been bestowed in an economical arrangement to save labor; which being an important point, is presumed will render the collection exceedingly useful to the cabinet-maker.

JOHN HALL,
Architect.

CONTENTS.

ALPHABETICALLY ARRANGED.

PRACTICAL PERSPECTIVE.

PLATE I.

FIGURE 1.—*To draw a cube or any rectangular figure in parallel perspective.*

Let *g. g.* be the ground line for the object to rest on; *H.H.* the horizon line drawn parallel to *g. g.* and five feet six inches above it.   This height being the standard for the horizon line for all objects that repose on a surface level with the spectator, draw the front of the object *a. a. a. a.*, determine on the vanishing point v. on the horizon line, and draw the angles of the front of the object to v.; determine on the distance you are stationed from the object, and place it equidistant from v. on the horizon line 1. 2. which are called the points of distance; draw a line from *a'.* to 2. and where it intersects the vanishing line *a. c".* defines the perspective square of the cube.   Raise a plumb line to the vanishing line above, and draw a

[B]

10

line at right angles to it, to meet the other vanishing line, and the exterior of the cube is completed; the dotted lines *c. c. c.* shows the back surface of the cube.   The point of distance 1. is not indispensable to draw the cube, but is shown for the purpose of knowing how to apply it to other objects, when required; one point of distance is sufficient to draw an object in this position.   The distance from *a.* to *d.* is equal to the front of the cube, and by drawing a line from *d.* to the point of distance p. d. 1., proves that the former intersections were correct.   A line drawn from a. to p. d. 1. touches the back angle of the cube at *c.* which completes the figure.   *Fig.* 2 is a similar object to *Fig.* 1.

FIG. 3.—*To draw an oblong figure in parallel perspective.*

Let it be desired to draw an object four feet long, one foot six inches high, and two feet wide. Draw the front of the figure *o. o. o. o.* to the required dimensions; set up five feet six inches by the same scale your object is drawn by, and draw the horizon line parallel to the ground line *g. g.*; determine on the vanishing point V. on the horizon line, and set off the point of distance from the vanishing point the same distance you are stationed from the object; measure off on the ground line from *o.* to *p.* the width of the object; draw the four angles of the front of the figure *o. o. o. o.* to the vanishing point *p.;* draw a line from *p.* on the ground to the point of distance, and where it intersects the bottom vanishing line determines the perspective square of the end; raise a perpendicular line to meet the vanishing line at *t.;* draw a line from *t.* parallel to the ground line to meet the vanishing line at *u.*, and the figure is completed.

PLATE I.

FIG. 4.—*To draw any figure whose top is inclined from a horizontal plane, such as the top of a writing desk, &c.*

Draw the front of the desk, *c. c. c. c.*, by the scale; raise the plumb line *c. w.* which is the measuring line for the perpendicular heights of the desk, both front and back; draw the horizon line five feet six inches from the ground line; fix on the vanishing point *van.* 1. at discretion; draw the vanishing line *c'.* to the vanishing point *van.* 1.; lay off the width of the desk from *c'.* to *b.* on the ground line; place the point of distance *dis.* from the vanishing point the same distance you stand from the object, and draw

b. to the point of distance, and where it intersects the bottom vanishing line defines the perspective square of the end; set up on the perpendicular measuring line the height you intend to have the desk behind, and draw from that height a line to the vanishing point *van.* 1.; raise a perpendicular from *a.* to meet the vanishing line *van.* 1.; draw a line from *c.* through *r.* and produce it to the horizon line, which gives the vanishing point for the top of the object. Draw a line at right angles to *a. r.* to meet the vanishing line at v. and the figure is completed.

PLATE I.

FIG. 5.—*To draw a writing desk, or box, with the lid thrown open to any required distance.*

Draw the front of the figure to the required size, and draw the perspective of the end in the same manner as the preceding figures. Take the width of the top and place it up from *e.* to *c.* on the perpendicular measuring line; draw a quarter of an oval from *g.* to *c.;* place the distance you intend to have the lid open from *e.* to *f.* and draw a line from *f.* to the vanishing point *van.* 1.; draw a line from *e.* through *h.*

and produce it to the horizon line *v. 2.*—then *v. 2.* is the vanishing point for the inclination of the top; draw a line to *h. i* and the figure is completed.

N. B. The top of this figure is perfectly level when let down; as for example, the top of a writing drawer of a secretary. The lid of a chest, when it opens from you, is drawn nearly in the same manner, only by reversing the curved line.

PLATE II.

FIG. 7.—*To draw any quantity of steps in parallel perspective.*

Draw the perpendicular measuring line *a. b.* and set up the heights of the steps 1. 2. 3. 4. &c.; then set off the number of steps on the ground line 1. 2. 3. &c.; draw the horizon line, and determine on the vanishing point *van.*; measure off the point of distance *dis.* from the vanishing point; draw lines from 1. 2. 3. 4. 5. 6. 7. on the vertical measuring line to the vanishing point; draw lines from the points 1. 2. 3. 4. 5. 6. on the ground line, to the point of distance to meet the bottom vanishing line, and from the points *d. c. e. f.*

g. h. raise plumb lines, which give the ends of the risers; commence with the bottom step by drawing a line from the right hand corner of the bottom riser to the vanishing point, then from *o.* the bottom of the second riser; draw a line parallel to the ground line to meet the vanishing line *x. x.* which gives the perspective square of the first step. Raise the second riser *o. x. x.* to meet the vanishing line, then from *w.* draw a line parallel to the former ones, which completes the second riser. Proceed on in the same way, until you have completed the whole of the risers and steps. The top *e. f. g. h.* is found in the same way as the steps, by setting off the width on the measuring ground line and drawing a line to the point of distance, the line *K. K.* goes off to the width of the platform on the ground line.

PLATE II.

FIG. 6.—*To find the perspective of an object when the vanishing point is directly over the centre of the object.*

Draw the front of the object *a. a. a. a.* and raise a vertical line in the centre of the figure to the horizon line for the vanishing point; fix on the point of distance from the vanishing point on the horizon line;

draw lines from the top corners of the front to the vanishing point; determine on the width of the figure, and set it off from *a.* to *b.* Draw a line from *b.* to the point of distance, and where it crosses the line *a. van.*, draw a line parallel to the front line, and the figure is completed.

N. B. In this case the width of the figure is half its length, but it can be drawn to any width by setting off the size from *a.* which will give the true perspective square of the top.

PLATE II.

Fɪɢ. 9.—*To draw a table in parallel perspective.*

Lay off the length and breadth of the table on the ground line, as *a. b.* for the length, and *b. c.* the width. Draw the horizon line five feet six inches above the ground line; determine on the vanishing point at discretion; also, the point of distance on the horizon line; draw *a.* and *b.* to the vanishing point, and *c.* to the point of distance; draw a line parallel to the front line from *d.* to *e.* which completes the perspective square for the four legs of the table to rest on; raise the legs on the corners of the perspective square,

the front legs must be drawn to their proper heights by the scale, and on those heights draw another perspective square, similar to the bottom one, which will form the top of the table; the figures 1. 2. 3. on the ground is the size of the legs, which drawn to the point of distance, gives the perspective of the legs.

PLATE II.

Fɪɢ. 8.—*To draw an object whose length is greater in front than behind, as the seats of chairs, &c.*

Draw the front of the figure *a. b. c. d.* and draw one of the corners to the vanishing point in the usual way, as for a right angled figure; determine on the width of the figure, which in this case is half its length; draw a line from *o.* to the point of distance, and where it intersects the outside vanishing line at *g.* is the perspective width of the object. Place half the distance you intend to have the figure shorter behind from *b.* to *f.* and draw a line from *f.* to the vanishing point; draw a line from *b.* to *i.* and produce it to the horizon line, which gives the point *van.* 2.; from *van.* 1. make *van.* 3. equal to *van.* 2. and draw the other end of the object to *van.* 3., which completes the figure.

17

PLATE III.

FIG. 10.—*To draw a hexagon or a pologon with six sides.*

A. shows the plan of the figure and method of drawing it; *B.* shows the figure drawn in parallel perspective. Carry up the angles of the plan *a. b. c. d.* to the ground line, and draw them to the vanishing point *o.;* set off from *e.* on the ground line the width of two of the sides of the figure, as 1. 2., and draw them to the point of distance; and where they intersect the vanishing line at 3. 4. draw lines to 5. 6. parallel to the ground line; draw a line from 8. to 4. and produce it to the horizon line *K.;* draw a line from 5. to *k.* and 8. 4., 5. 6. are two sides of the figure; draw a line from 4. to 9. and produce it to the horizon line at *i.;* make a line from 7. to *i.* and the figure is finished.

[c]

18

PLATE III.

FIG. 11.—*To draw an octagon or a pologon with eight sides.*

A. shows the plan of the figure and method of drawing it; *B.* shows the figure in parallel perspective. Carry up the sides of the figure *a. b. c. d.* to the ground line, and draw them to the vanishing point *o.;* lay off the sides of the figure *e. f. g.* on the ground line; determine on the point of distance you are stationed from the object, and measure it off from the vanishing point on the horizon line; draw *e. f. g. h. i. j.* to the point of distance, *h. k. l. m.* gives the perspective square of the plane; *f. s.* cuts off one corner of the perspective square for one side of the figure, and *j. s.* another corner. Draw a line from *i.* to *u.* and produce it to the horizon line at *x.;* draw another line from *w.* to *x.* and the figure is completed.

PLATE III.

Fɪɢ. 12.—*To construct a vanishing circle.*

Take 5. 4. for the base line, 2. 0. being the vanishing line, in the centre of the base line; this being the best position for the vanishing point to draw a perspective circle, find the perspective square of the circle as 4. 5. 6. 7.; draw the diagonals, and through their intersections draw the line *a. b.* parallel to the base line; divide the base line into four equal parts, and draw 1. *a.* and 3. *b.* which gives the points *c. d.;* draw lines from *c. d.* to the vanishing point, and they will give the points *f. e.;* so that the eight points, *a. b. c. d. e. f.* 2. 8. will be the points for the circle to be drawn to.

Rᴇᴍᴀʀᴋs. When it is not convenient for want of room, to have the whole point of distance from the vanishing point, the perspective square of any object may be found by taking half the distance from the vanishing point, and half of the base of the figure as shown at 2. on the base line and *dis.* ½ on the horizon line.

PLATE IV.

Fɪɢ. 13.—*To construct a right angled figure in oblique or angular perspective.*

Let *A. B.* be the measuring line for the base of the figure, *o. p.* the perpendicular measuring line and angle of the figure; from *o.* lay off the length 1. 2. 3. 4. feet, the length by the scale, and 1. 2. 3. the width of the figure; determine on the two vanishing points, and draw *o. p.* to those points; fix on the distance you are from the object, at *S.* the stationed point; let fall the vanishing points, plumb to the measuring line, and from those points as centres, and with the radius *A. S.* and *B. S.*, describe the segments *S. K.* and *B. i.*, which gives the points *i. K.*, on the measuring line; carry those points up to the horizon line, and they are the points of distance. To cut off the length and breadth for the perspective squares, draw lines from 3. 8. and 4. 9., and where they intersect the vanishing lines at 5. 6., raise plumb lines to meet the top vanishing lines at 7. *x.;* draw 7. *x.* to the vanishing points, and the figure is completed.

PLATE V.

MOULDINGS.

Plate V. shows the principal mouldings which are used in cabinet furniture, with their architectural characters, and methods of drawing them.   These examples are of the most simple kind, being formed of concentric curves.   Where gracefulness of outline is required in mouldings, or scroll work, they should partake of the elliptical curve, which is the predominant feature in Grecian ornament, and decidedly the most beautiful that can be adopted.   The Geometric mode of drawing Grecian mouldings has been omitted in the present work, in consequence of their complex nature; but the variety of scrolls and the simple method of drawing them, with elliptical curves, exhibited in a subsequent part of this work, will be deemed sufficient to enable any workman by a very little practice, to draw any ornament of any description.

22

PLATE VI.

CORNICES.

Figure 24 is a cornice for a wardrobe, book-case or any piece of furniture, sufficiently elevated to raise it above the eye.   Fig. 25 is a cornice for a similar purpose as the foregoing figure; but of a different pattern.   The curve part of both figures are of Grecian outline, that of figure 24 is termed a Grecian echinus, and that of figure 25 a Grecian ogee, or cyma recta.   Fig. 27 is a profile of a consol or truss for a pilaster wardrobe.   Fig. 26 the front view of the consol.

PLATE VII.

CORNICES.

Figs. 28 and 29 are two examples, for cornices of wardrobes, or any other piece of furniture they may be adapted for.   Figs. 30 and 31 are a front and side view of a consol to support the above cornices.

Those consols and the preceding ones, although their outlines are broken, are peculiarly adapted for the present style of work, as their fronts are capable of being veneered or carved as taste may require.

PLATE VIII.

CORNICES.

Figs. 32 and 33, are designed for cornices for wardrobes of a more expensive description than the preceding ones. Figs. 34 and 35, are a profile and front view of a truss for a wardrobe or any thing else it may be adapted for.

PLATE IX.

BED PILLARS.

Figs 36, 37, 38, and 39, are four designs for bed pillars; they are adapted for plain pillars or they are forms that are susceptible of being carved as taste may dictate.

PLATE X.

SCROLLS.

This Plate shows the method of drawing scrolls of any description in the most simple manner. Let it be desired to draw a consol for a pier-table, Fig. 40; draw a plumb line *a. b.* for the back of the scroll; determine on the height and draw *b. c.* and *a. d.* at right angles to *a. b.*; draw the line *c. e.* parallel to *a. b.* for the projection of the scroll at the top, also *d. f.* the projection at the bottom; determine on the depth and width of the revolving parts of the scroll, and draw lines in like manner to the former ones. Commence at the top to draw the scroll by dotting a line with a piece of chalk to touch the straight lines at the most prominent parts of the scroll; when you have made a graceful line with the chalk, take a soft lead pencil and go over those dots correcting at the same time any inaccuracies that may present themselves; when this is done, you have a pattern lined out of the exact dimensions you required. The whole of the following figures on Plate X. may be drawn in the same manner as figure 40.

PLATE XI.

CONSOLS.

The whole of these figures are fac-similes of plate X. with the exception of their being finished examples. Figs. 50 and 51, are patterns of consols for pier-tables, drawn a twelfth part of full size. Figs. 56 and 59 are scrolls for pier-tables. Figs. 52 to 55, are feet for pier-tables or any other job they may be adapted for. Figs. 53, 57 and 58, are patterns of consols for smaller jobs, such as wash-stands, secretaries, &c.

PLATE XII.

CONSOLS.

Figs. 60 to 63, are four designs for consols of pier-tables drawn to a scale of one inch to a foot or a twelfth part of full size. Figs. 64 to 68 are five different patterns for various purposes, drawn to the scale affixed to the plate. The whole of these scrolls are adapted to the present plain style of work.

[D]

They are forms also that are equally capable of receiving profuse ornament, if required. Any of these scrolls can be drawn by attending to the rules laid down for plate X. If it be required to copy the proportions of these scrolls, it can be done by referring to the scale accompanying each plate, and increasing the size of them to any required dimensions.

PLATE XIII.

PLATFORMS.

Figs. 69 to 74, are six designs for platforms for pier-tables, wash-stands, toilet-tables, &c. drawn to the scale that accompanies them.

PLATE XIV.

PLATFORMS.

Figs. 75 to 80, are six different patterns for platforms of pier-tables and various other articles of furniture.

PLATE XV.

PIER-TABLES.

Figs. 81 and 82 are two end views of pier-tables, drawn to a scale of one inch to a foot.

PLATE XVI.

PIER-TABLES.

Figs. 83 and 84 are two end views for designs of pier-tables, drawn to the scale that accompanies them.

PLATE XVII.

PIER-TABLES.

Figs. 85 and 86 are two designs for pier-tables, drawn in perspective to a scale of one inch to a foot. The consols of Fig. 85 are the same pattern as Fig. 81.   The feet are the same pattern as shown at Fig. 54.   The consols of Fig. 86 are the same pattern as Fig. 50.

PLATE XVIII.

SCROLLS.

Figs. 87 to 97, are eleven different patterns of scrolls for toilet-tables, wash-stands, and a variety of other purposes, to which they may be applied.   The whole of these scrolls can be drawn to any size, by following the principles laid down for plate X.

PLATE XIX.

PLATFORMS FOR CENTRE TABLES.

Fig. 98 shows a platform for a centre table.   Draw one-eighth part of the platform as indicated by the line 1. 2. and it will answer to draw the whole of the platform.   Fig. 100 shows three different patterns for a platform of a centre table.   To draw the pattern *A.* carry out the line 1. 0. at right angles to 1. 4. and 2. 0. at right angles to 2. 3. and where they intersect at 0. is the centre for the curve; draw the eighth part of the platform, as *B.* and *C.*, and it will answer for the whole.   The geometrical method of drawing *B.* and *C.* is not shown here for the same reasons assigned in plate V. relative to Grecian mouldings, those curves being formed of parts of an oval, would be too intricate for the artizan to attend to their geometrical construction; the practitioner will soon acquire a taste for graceful lines by attending to the following items: First, never to use the compasses to produce an oval form, or any part of it; secondly, never to join two circles, of different radii, to form a scroll.   Endeavor to acquire a freedom of hand, by drawing those elliptical lines to be pleasing to the eye.   Figs. 99 and 101, are two patterns for feet for centre-tables; by increasing their heights they may be applied to sofas.

PILLARS.

Figs. 102 to 105 are patterns for centre-table pillars, which can be made square, octagon or with any other number of sides.

PLATE XX.

PLATFORMS.

Figs 106 and 107 are two patterns for table platforms.   The sides *A. D. C.* of Fig. 106 are drawn in the same manner as described at *A.*, Fig. 100.   The side *B.* is of the same form, but the method of

finding the centre for the curve is different.   Determine on the depth you want the side cut out from *a.* to *b.* besect *c. d.* at *a.* and draw *a. b.* at right angles to *c. d.*, draw *c. b.* and *b. d.*, besect *c. b.* and *b. d.* at 1. 2., and draw lines at right angles to *b. d.* and *b. c.* at 1. 2. and where they intersect each other will be the centre for the curve.

Fig. 107 is a platform for an end table.   To draw this platform, lay out the square of the length and breadth, besect the width at 1. and draw the line 1. 6. at right angles to *w. x.*, place the distance *x.* 1. to *x.* 5. and draw 5. 6. at right angles to 5. *x.*; draw the diagonal 6. *x.*, cut off the corner 3. 4. at right angles to *x.* 6., determine on the depth of the curve and find the centre, to draw the segment as laid down in Fig. 106, or it may be obtained as indicated by the line *d. g.*; to obtain this line, place one leg of the compasses on *a.* and with any radius more than half the distance from *a.* to *c.* describe the arc *h. g.* then place one leg of the compasses with the same radius on *c.* and cross the former arc, through those intersections draw the line *d. g.*; a line found in the same way on the other half of the segment and drawn to intersect each other, will give the centre for the curve.   To draw the end curve make the depth 1. 2. the same as 1. 2. on the side; commence by dotting the form with a piece of chalk to meet the three points 0. 2. 3., observing that the outer part of the curve terminates in a parallel direction with the line *x.* 6.; when you have gotten the dotted line to please, finish the line with a lead pencil.   The half pattern shown at *C.* will answer for the whole.

Figs. 108 to 111, are four patterns for table pillars.   Fig. 108 has eight sides; the others are four square.

PLATE XXI.

CENTRE TABLES.

Figs. 112 and 113, are two designs for centre tables, shown in perspective.   Fig. 112 has a four square pillar, and that of the other an eight square pillar.

PLATE XXII.

SOFA FEET.

Figs. 114 to 123 are nine patterns for sofa feet, the forms are various, and most of them susceptible of being highly ornamented with carving, if taste should require it.

PLATE XXIII.

SOFA ENDS.

Figs. 124 to 133, are various patterns for sofa ends, which can be made plain or ornamented, with carving as it may be required.   Figs. 124 to 129 are a variety of patterns for sofa feet.   Fig. 128 is the front view of Fig. 129.

PLATE XXIV.

SOFA ENDS.

Figs. 130 and 131 are two designs for sofa ends.   Figs. 132 to 135, are patterns for upright sofa ends; the consols are adapted for carving, if required.

PLATE XXV.

SOFAS.

Figs. 138 and 139 are two designs for sofas.   Fig. 138 has upright or square ends, that of Fig. 139 has scroll ends.

CHAIRS.

Figs. 136 and 137 are two designs for chair backs.

PLATE XXVI.

SOFAS.

Fig. 140 is a design for a sofa with upright ends; the pattern of the end of this sofa is the same as Fig. 130.   Figs. 141 to 143 are designs for footstools.

[E]

PLATE XXVII.

LOUNGUES.

Figs. 144 and 145 are two designs for lounges.

CHAIRS.

Fig. 146 is a design for a parlor chair.

PLATE XXVIII.

RECLINING CHAIRS.

Fig. 147 is an easy chair, it may be covered with morocco, or velvet, with tufts; and is quite easy to sit on.

Fig. 148 is a view of a reclining chair for an invalid; the position of the back of this chair can be varied at pleasure, and the projecting part in front can be elongated and adjusted to any angle with the seat.   When it is required to be used as an easy chair, the back can be fixed upright, and the front projection slid in, so as to have the appearance of a common easy chair.

PLATE XXIX.

HALL CHAIRS.

Figs. 149 and 150 are two designs for hall chairs, they are constructed entirely of wood.

PLATE XXX.

WORK TABLES.

Figs. 151 and 152 are two designs for ladies work tables.   A sliding top pulls out from underneath the maintop of Fig. 152 to hold a candle, &c.

PLATE XXXI.

LADIES' WORK TABLES.

Fig. 154 is a design for a lady's work table drawn in perspective.   Fig. 153 is the end view of Fig. 154.   Fig. 155 is another end view of rather a different pattern.

PLATE XXXII.

TABLES.

Fig. 156 is a design for a card table with a square pillar.   Fig. 157 is a design for an end table with an octagonal pillar.

PLATE XXXIII.

TABOURETTES.

Figs. 158 to 163 are end views of tabourettes or stools, all of them drawn to the scale affixed to the plate.

PLATE XXXIV.

TABOURETTES.

Figs. 164 to 169 are six designs for tabourettes drawn to a scale of an inch to a foot, many of those scrolls are of novel description, and may be applied to various purposes with great advantage.

PLATE XXXV.

BUREAUS.

Fig. 171 is a design for a consol bureau.   Fig. 170 is the end view of Fig. 171.

PLATE XXXVI.

TOILETTE TABLE.

Fig. 172 is a design for a toilette table, the consols are the same pattern as Fig. 59, the pediment ornament the same pattern as Fig. 194.

DRESSING BUREAUS.

Fig. 173 is a design for a dressing bureau.

PLATE XXXVII.

WARDROBES.

Figs. 174 and 175 are two designs for wardrobes.   Fig. 175 is a winged wardrobe with a dressing bureau in the centre.   The glass is supported by the pillars, the pillars resting on a marble slab, and they are independent of the wings.   The doors of the wings may open on the front or ends as may be most convenient for the place on which it is to stand.

PLATE XXXVIII.

FRENCH BEDSTEADS.

Figs. 176 to 180 are designs for the scroll ends and posts of French bedsteads.

PLATE XXXIX.

BOOK CASE DOORS.

Figs. 181 to 183 are three designs for book case doors, there may be a little carving put about Figs. 181 and 182, or they may be executed quite plain, as the whole of the ornamental parts can be formed of fillets; their ends terminating in scrolls.

PLATE XL.

SECRETARIA BOOK CASES.

Figs. 184 and 185 are two designs for secretaria book cases. Fig. 185 has a drawer which pulls out, and the front of the drawer falls down and is supported with a quadrant at each end for the purpose of writing on. The interior is fitted up with drawers and pidgeon holes. Fig. 185 is much lower than the preceding one; the doors have mirrors in them. The writing drawer pulls out to nearly its whole depth, and has a writing top that is hinged in front, and can be adjusted, by a rack underneath the top, to any angle required; at each end of the writing drawer there are receptacles for pens, ink, &c.

PLATE XLI.

PEDESTALS.

Figs. 186 and 187 are two designs for pedestals or side boards, it is best for the doors to open on the ends. They can be made with or without drawers on the top, and to open on the front or ends.

PLATE XLII.

MUSIC STOOLS.

Figs. 188 to 190 are three designs for music or piano stools. Fig. 188 has a chair back. The whole of the seats raises from the stands by turning round the top, which raise a screw that works in a nut contained in the pillar. The screw is sometimes made of wood, but iron is preferable, as working better and lasting longer.

PLATE XLIII.

ORNAMENTS.

Figs. 191 to 198 are designs for pediment ornaments, which can be made with flat surfaces and veneered and relieved with a little carving, as shown in the figures. Or they are forms that are adapted for being superbly carved, if required.

REMARKS. The whole of those ornaments can be drawn by following the rules laid down for drawing scroll work in plate X. By drawing one half of the ornament on paper or wood for a pattern, by turning it over, it will answer for the other half.

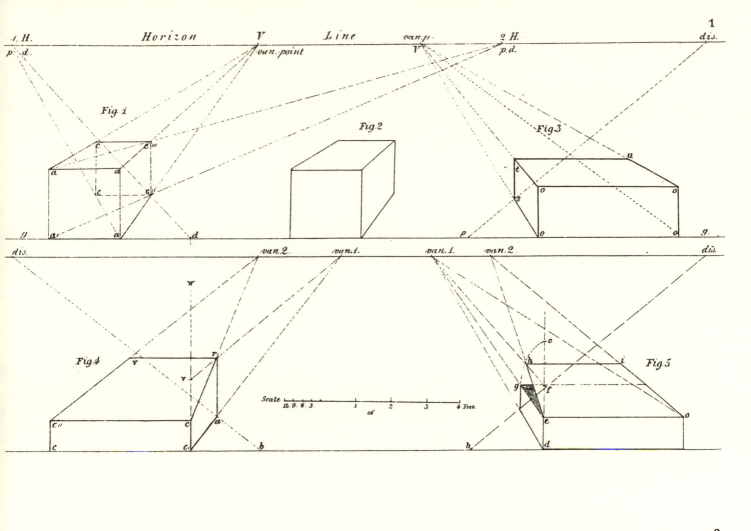

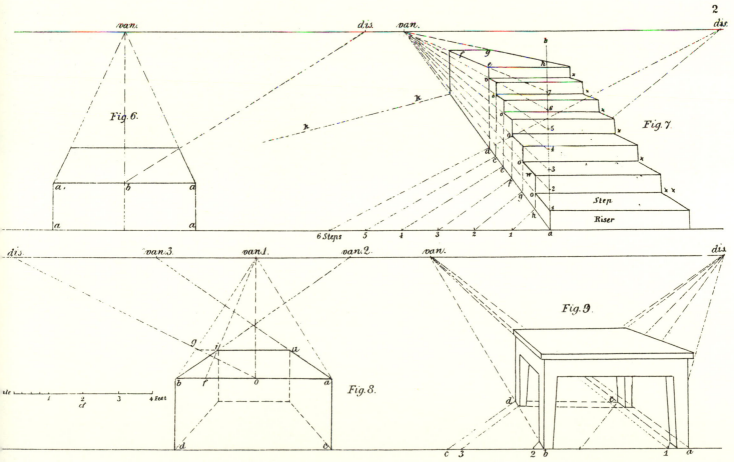

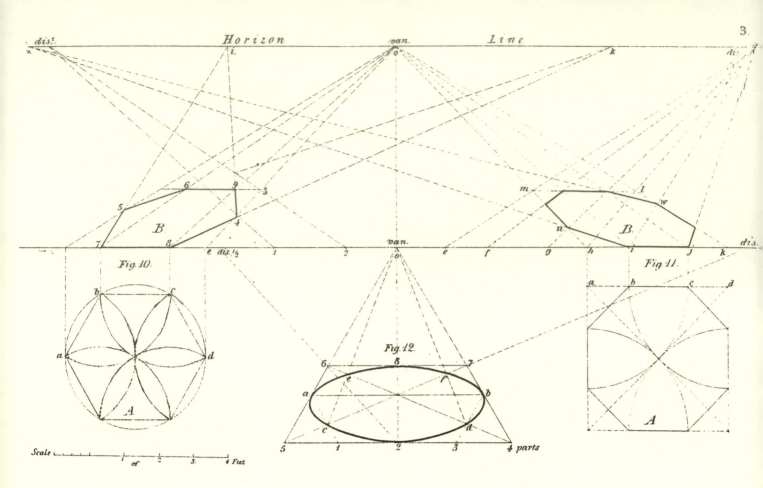

dis.ᵗ   Horizon   van.   Line   dis.ᵗ

x   i   o   k   dis. A

6   9   3

5   m   l   w

B   n   B   dis.

7   8   e dis.½   1   2   van.   e   f   g   h   i   j   k   dis.

Fig. 10.   van.   Fig. 11.

b   c   a   b   c   d

a   d   8   7

Fig. 12.   e   f

a   b

A   c   d   A

Scale _____ of   1   2   3   4 Feet   5   1   2   3   4 parts

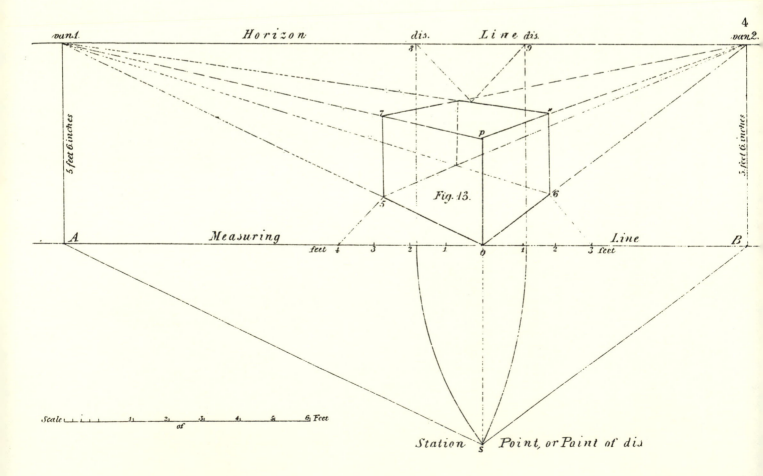

van.1   Horizon   dis.   Line dis.   van.2

8   9

5 feet 6 inches   7   r   5 feet 6 inches

p

5   6

A   Measuring   Fig. 13.   Line   B

feet 4   3   2   1   0   1   2   3 feet

Scale _____ of   1   2   3   4   5   6 Feet

Station   Point, or Point of dis

s

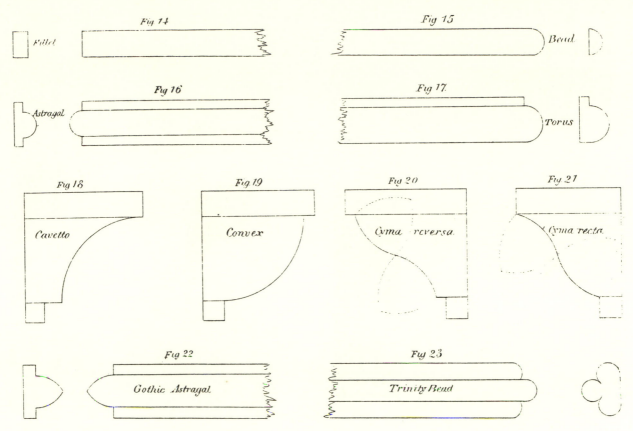

Fig 14
Fillet
Fig 15
Bead

Fig 16
Astragal
Fig 17
Torus

Fig 18
Cavetto
Fig 19
Convex
Fig 20
Cyma reversa
Fig 21
Cyma recta

Fig 22
Gothic Astragal
Fig 23
Trinity Bead

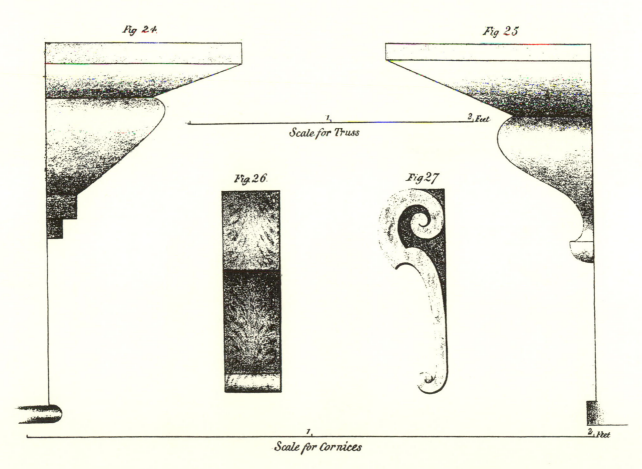

Fig 24.
Fig 25
1   2 Feet
Scale for Truss

Fig 26.
Fig 27

1   2 Feet
Scale for Cornices

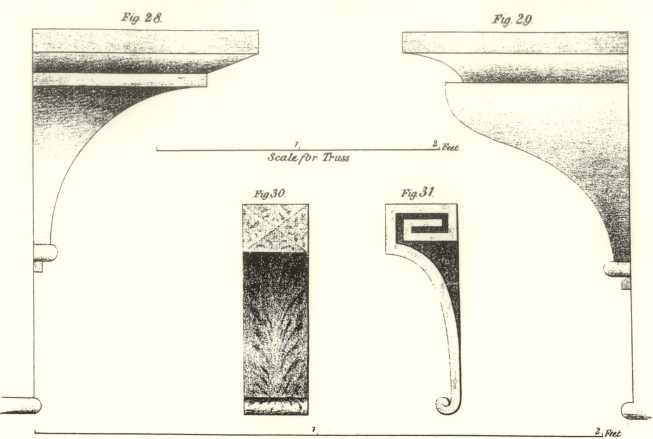

Fig. 28.

Fig. 29.

Scale for Truss

Fig. 30.

Fig. 31.

Scale for Cornices

8

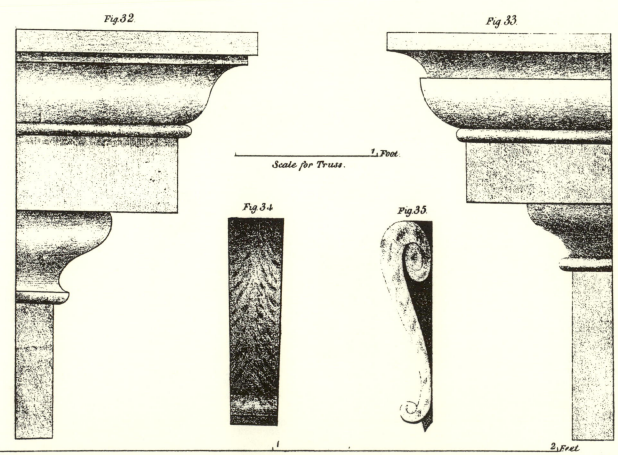

Fig. 32.

Fig. 33.

Scale for Truss.

Fig. 34.

Fig. 35.

Scale for Cornices

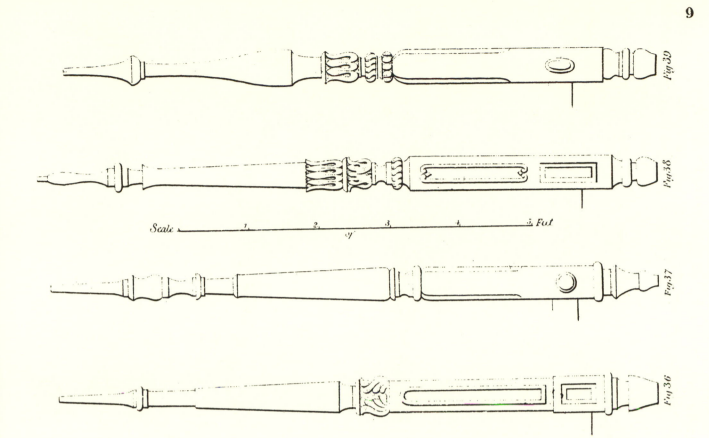

Fig 39

Fig 38

Scale   1   2   3   4   5 Feet
or

Fig 37

Fig 36

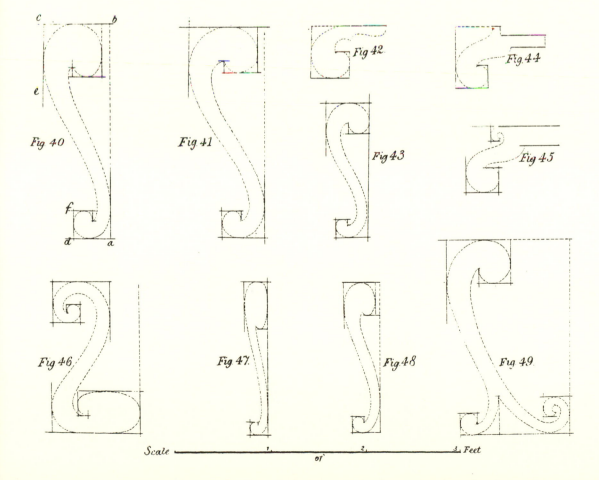

Fig 42

Fig 44

Fig 40

Fig 41

Fig 43

Fig 45

Fig 46

Fig 47

Fig 48

Fig 49

Scale   1   2   3 Feet
or

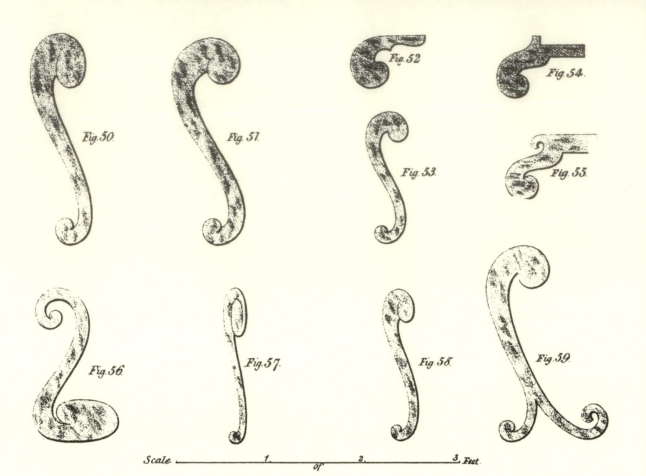

Fig. 50.   Fig. 51.   Fig. 52   Fig. 54.

Fig. 53.   Fig. 55.

Fig. 56.   Fig. 57.   Fig. 58.   Fig. 59.

Scale ———————— 1. —of— 2. ————————— 3. Feet.

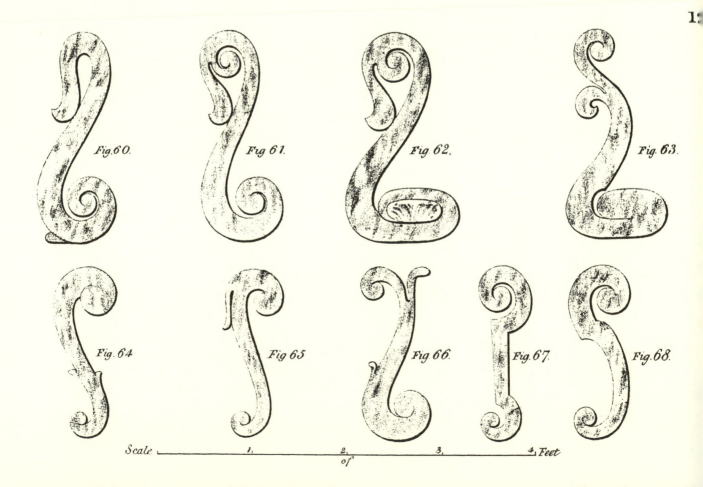

Fig. 60.   Fig. 61.   Fig. 62.   Fig. 63.

Fig. 64.   Fig. 65.   Fig. 66.   Fig. 67.   Fig. 68.

Scale ———————— 1. —of— 2. ————————— 3. ————————— 4. Feet

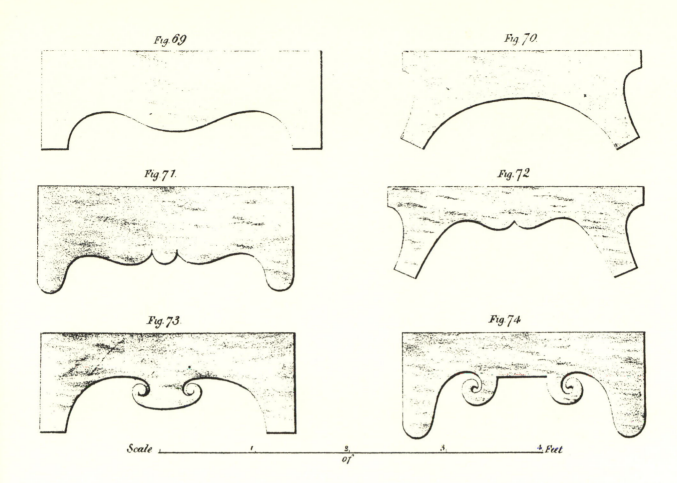

Fig.69

Fig.70

Fig.71

Fig.72

Fig.73

Fig.74

Scale of

1   2   3   4 Feet

Fig.75

Fig.76

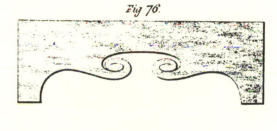

Fig.77

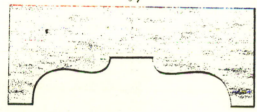

Fig.78

Fig.79

Fig.80

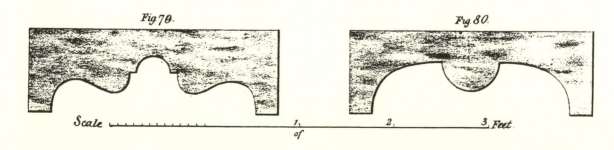

Scale of

1   2   3 Feet

Fig. 81.

Fig. 82.

Scale |||||||||||||||| 1, 2, Feet
of.

Fig 83

Fig 84

Scale ||||||||||||| 1, 2, 3, Feet
of

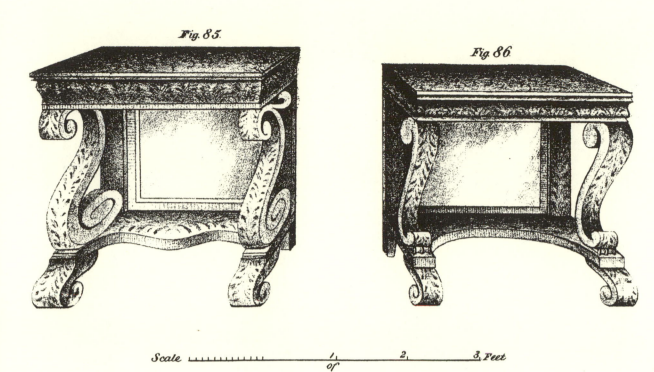

Fig. 85.

Fig. 86.

Scale |⊥⊥⊥⊥⊥⊥⊥⊥⊥⊥⊥————————1⁄of————————2.————————3. Feet

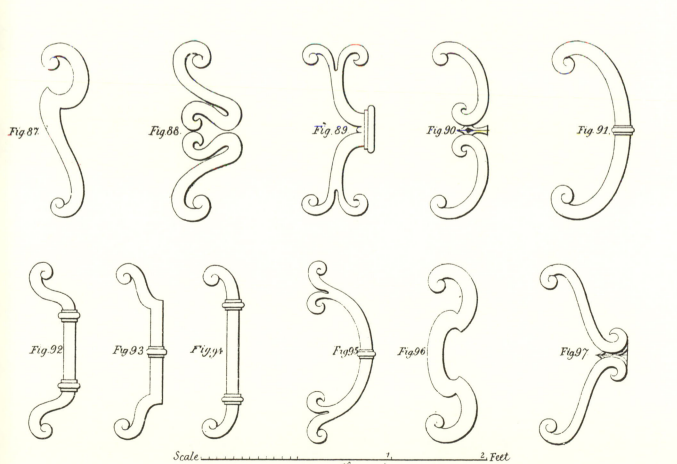

Fig. 87.   *Fig. 88.*   *Fig. 89.*   *Fig. 90.*   *Fig. 91.*

Fig. 92   *Fig. 93.*   *Fig. 94.*   *Fig. 95.*   *Fig. 96.*   *Fig. 97.*

Scale |⊥⊥⊥⊥⊥⊥⊥⊥⊥⊥————————1⁄of————————2. Feet

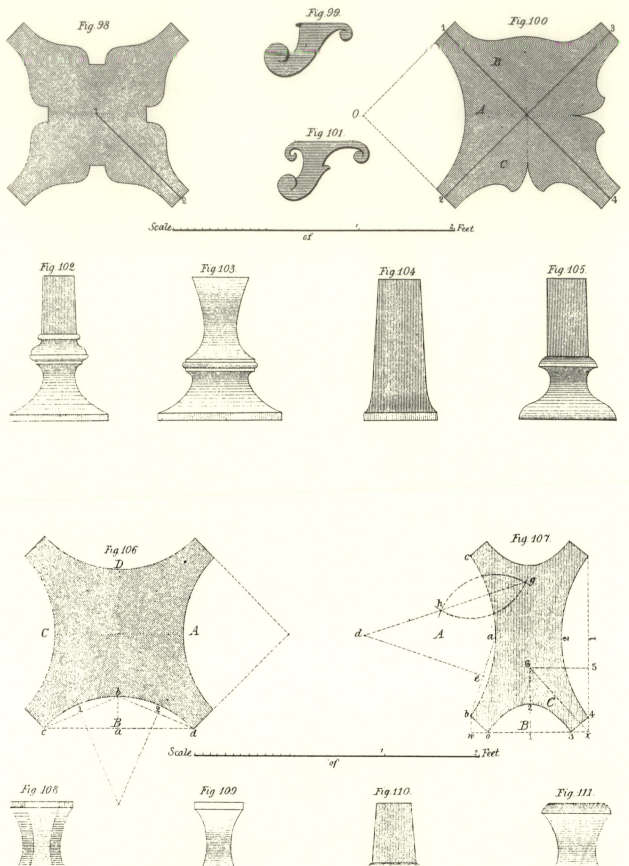

Fig. 98

Fig. 99.

Fig. 100

Fig. 101.

Scale ————————————— Feet
of

Fig. 102.

Fig. 103.

Fig. 104.

Fig. 105.

Fig. 106

Fig. 107.

Scale ————————————— Feet
of

Fig. 108.

Fig. 109.

Fig. 110.

Fig. 111.

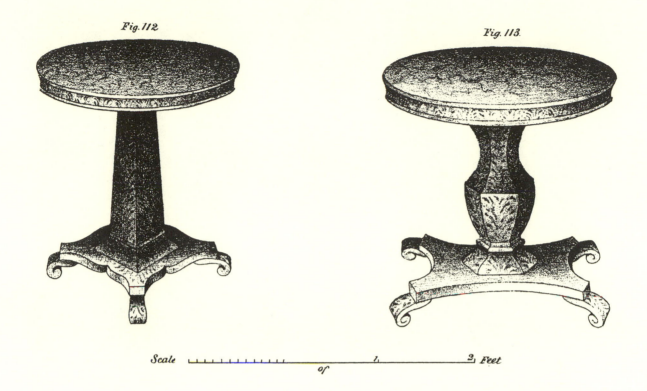

Fig. 112

Fig. 113

Scale ⊢————————————⊣ *of* ╵1 ╵2 *Feet*

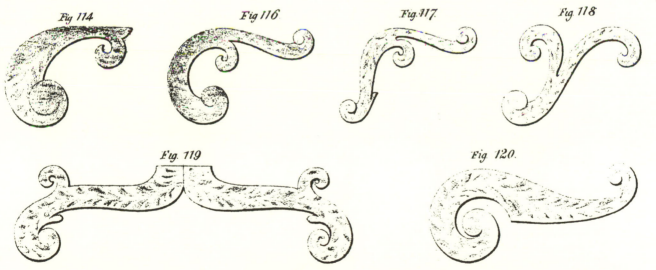

Fig 114

Fig 116

Fig. 117

Fig. 118

Fig. 119

Fig. 120

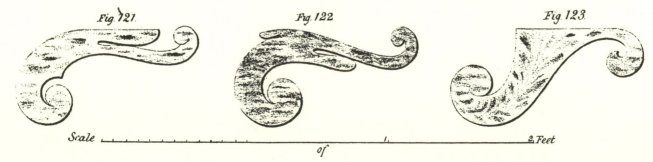

Fig. 121

Fig. 122

Fig. 123

Scale ⊢————————————⊣ *of* ╵1 ╵2 *Feet*

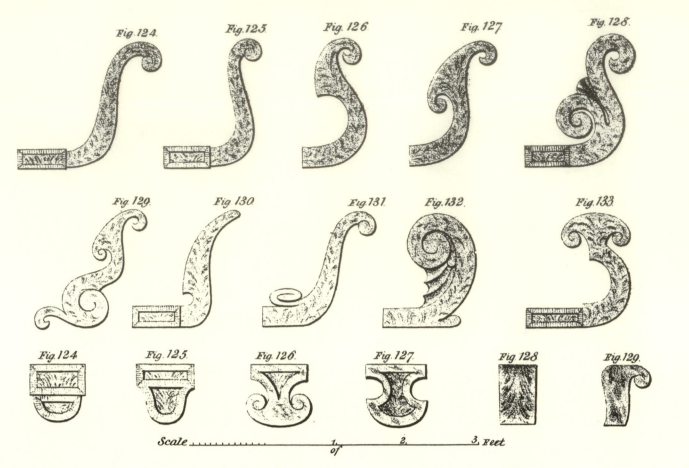

Fig. 124. Fig. 125. Fig. 126. Fig. 127 Fig. 128.

Fig. 129. Fig. 130 Fig. 131. Fig. 132. Fig. 133

Fig. 124 Fig. 125. Fig. 126. Fig. 127. Fig. 128 Fig. 129.

Scale of 1 2 3 Feet

Scale of 1 2 Feet

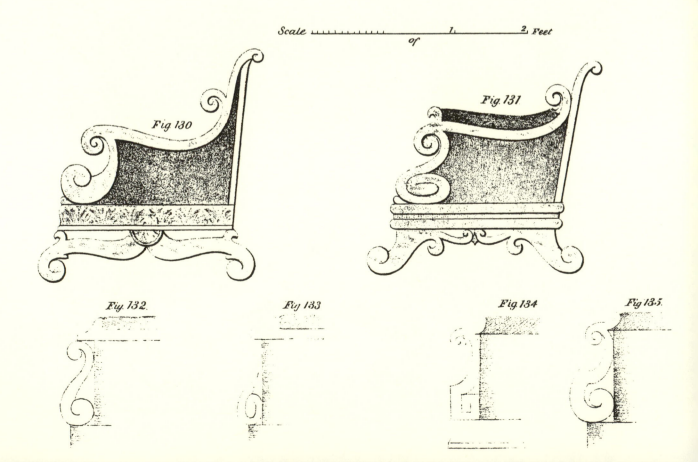

Fig. 130

Fig. 131

Fig. 132. Fig. 133 Fig. 134. Fig. 135.

Fig. 136.

Fig. 138.

Fig. 137.

Fig. 139.

26.

Fig. 140.

Scale _____ 1 ___ 2 ___ 3. Feet
of

Fig. 142.

Fig. 141.

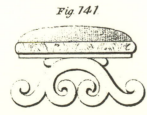

Fig. 143.

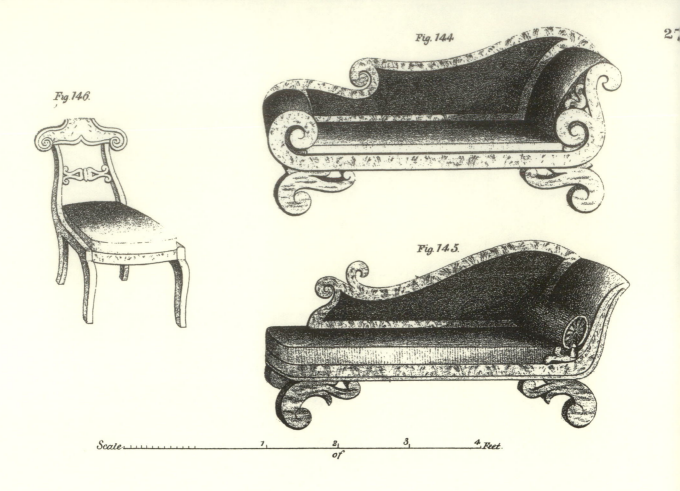

Fig. 144.

Fig. 146.

Fig. 145.

Scale ||||||||||| 1 2 3 4 Feet.
of

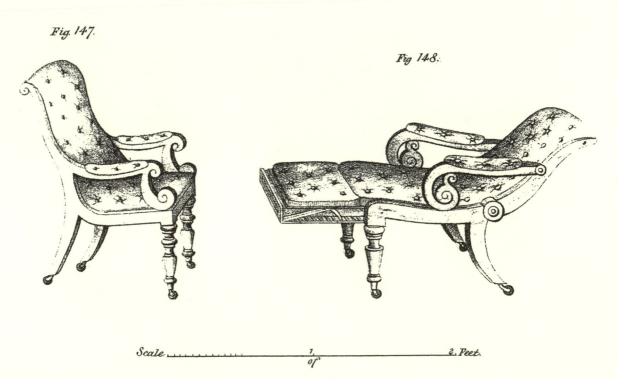

Fig. 147.

Fig 148.

Scale ||||||||||| 1 2 Feet.
of

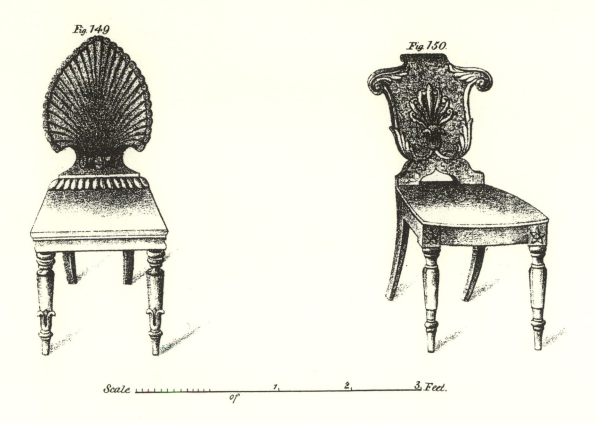

Fig. 149

Fig. 150.

Scale of 1 2 3 Feet.

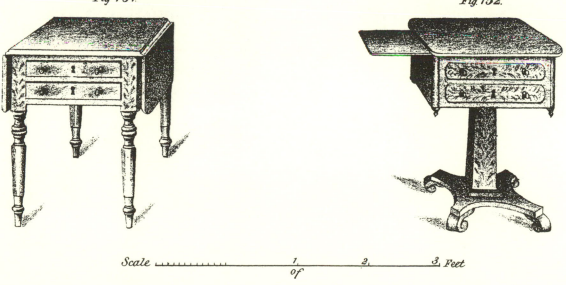

Fig 151.

Fig. 152.

Scale of 1 2 3 Feet

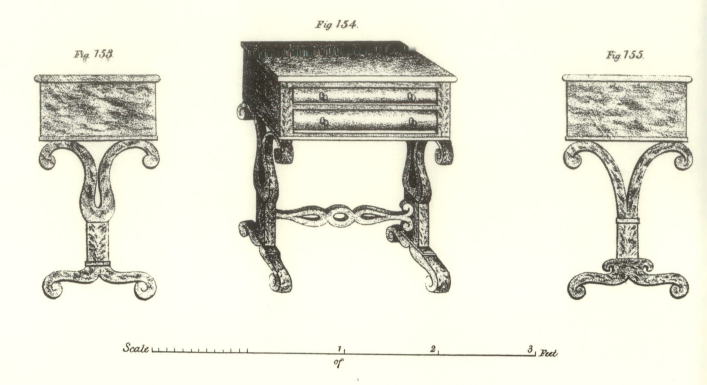

Fig 153.   Fig 154.   Fig 155.

Scale |⎯⎯⎯⎯⎯⎯⎯⎯⎯⎯⎯⎯⎯⎯⎯⎯ 1 ⎯⎯⎯⎯⎯⎯⎯⎯ 2 ⎯⎯⎯⎯⎯⎯⎯⎯ 3 Feet
       of

Fig. 156.   Fig. 157.

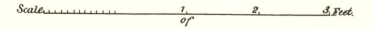

Scale |⎯⎯⎯⎯⎯⎯⎯⎯⎯⎯⎯⎯ 1 ⎯⎯⎯⎯⎯⎯⎯ 2 ⎯⎯⎯⎯⎯ 3 Feet.
       of

Fig. 158.

Fig.159.

Fig. 160.

Fig. 161.

Fig. 162.

Fig. 163

Scale ⊢┼┼┼┼┼┼┼┼┼┼┼───────────────── 1, ────────── 2, ────────── 3, Feet
of

Fig. 164.

Fig. 165.

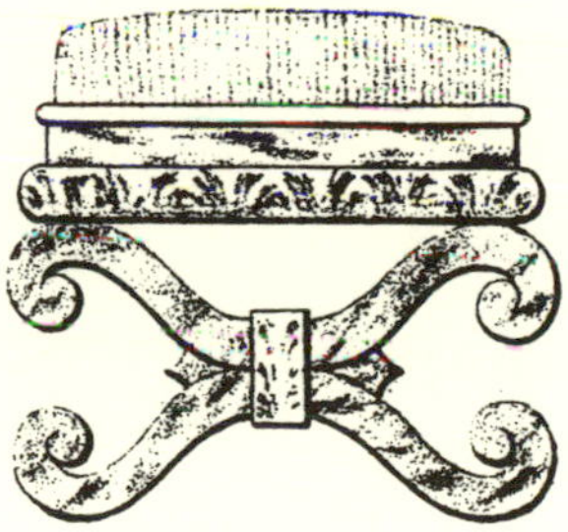

Fig. 166.

Fig. 167.

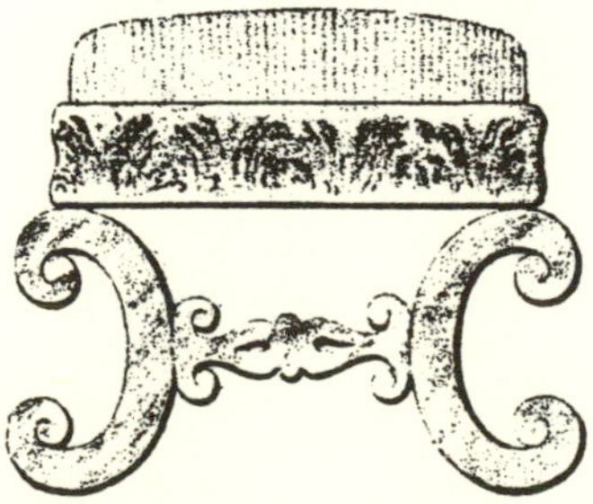

Fig. 168.

Fig. 169.

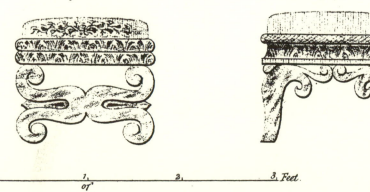

Scale ⊢┼┼┼┼┼┼┼┼┼┼┼───────────────── 1, ────────── 2, ────────── 3, Feet.
of

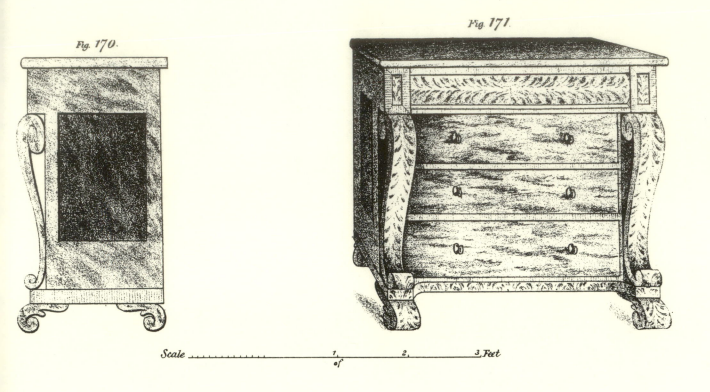

Fig. 170.

Fig. 171.

Scale .... 1 2 3 Feet
of

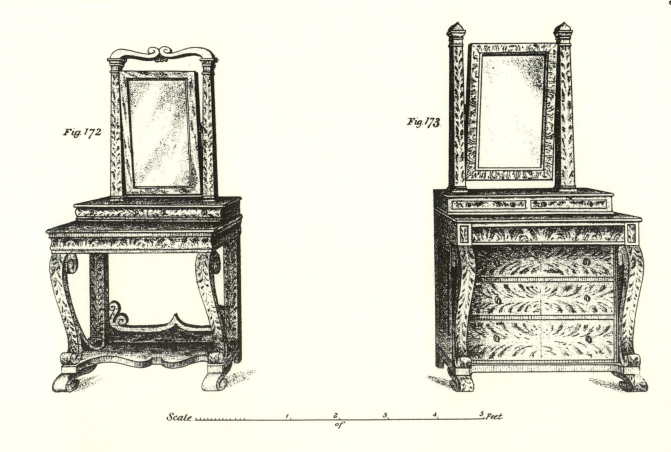

Fig. 172

Fig. 173.

Scale .... 1 2 3 4 5 Feet
of

Fig. 174

Fig. 175

Scale ||||||||| 1, 2, 3, 4, 5, 6, 7, Feet
of

Fig. 176. Fig. 177. Fig. 178. Fig. 179. Fig. 180

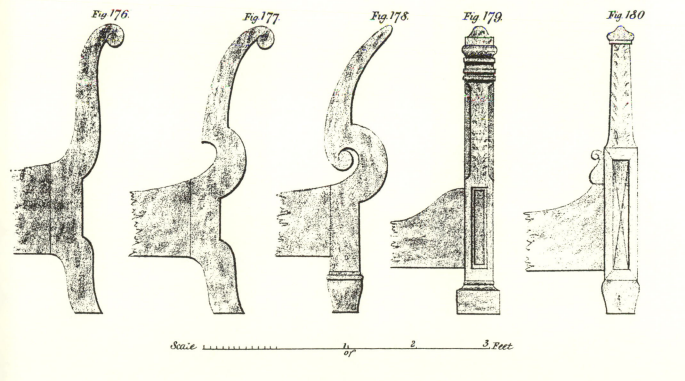

Scale ||||||||| 1, 2, 3, Feet
of

Fig. 181 Fig. 182 Fig. 183.

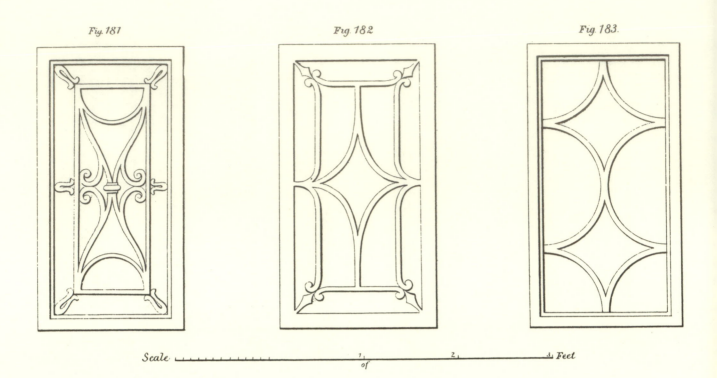

Scale |... 1, ... 2, ... 3. Feet
of

Fig. 184

Fig. 185.

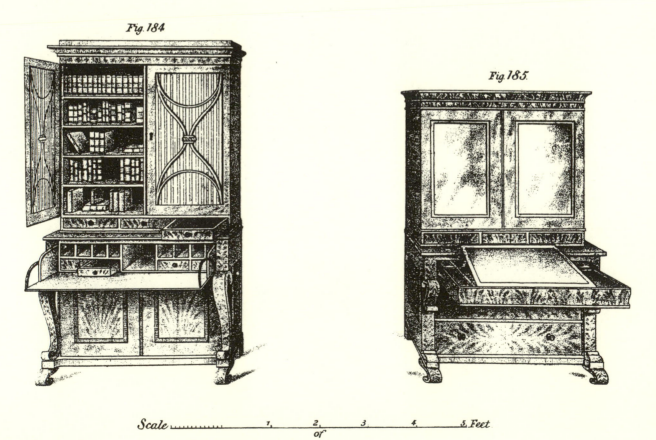

Scale |............ 1, ... 2, ... 3, ... 4, ... 5. Feet
of

Fig 186.

Fig. 187.

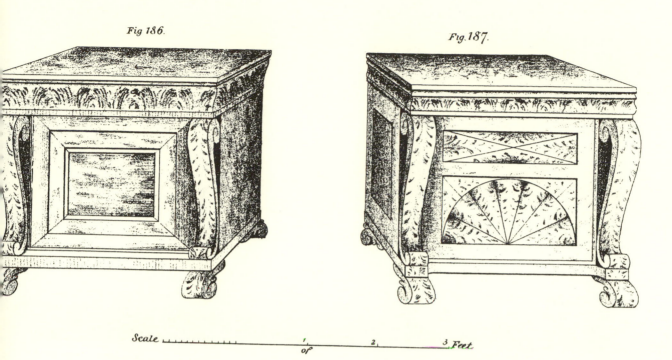

Scale ⊢⊣⊢⊣⊢⊣⊢⊣⊢⊣———————— 1 ————— 2 ———— 3 Feet
of

Fig. 188.

Fig. 189.

Fig. 190.

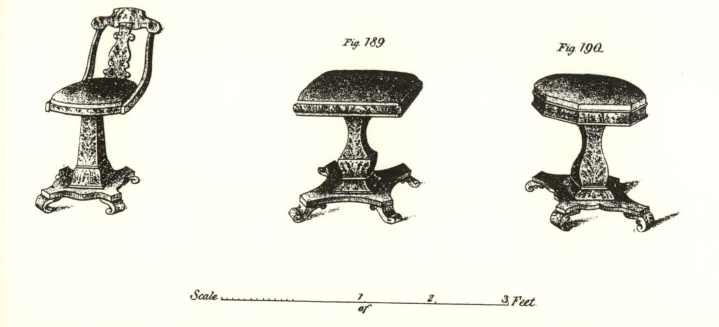

Scale ⊢⊣⊢⊣⊢⊣⊢⊣⊢⊣———————— 1 ————— 2 ———— 3 Feet.
of

Fig. 191.

Fig. 192.

Fig. 193.

Fig. 194.

Fig. 195.

Fig. 196.

Fig. 197.

Fig. 198.

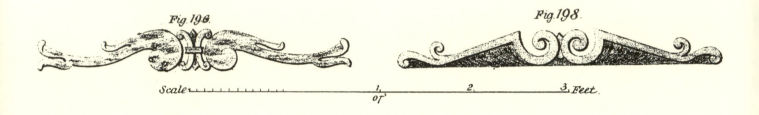

Scale ⊢⊢⊢⊢⊢⊢⊢⊢⊢⊢ 1 2 3 Feet.
                    10

A SERIES

OF

SELECT AND ORIGINAL

MODERN DESIGNS

FOR

DWELLING HOUSES,

FOR THE USE OF

CARPENTERS AND BUILDERS:

ADAPTED TO THE

Style of Building in the United States:

WITH TWENTY-FOUR PLATES.

By JOHN HALL, Architect,

AUTHOR OF THE CABINET MAKERS' ASSISTANT, &c.

BALTIMORE:

PRINTED BY JOHN MURPHY, 146 MARKET STREET.

::::::::::::::

1840.

PREFACE.

In presenting to the public a treatise on this delightful and important subject, the undersigned cannot but flatter himself, that he will produce something that will be useful to every person connected with the building art. In this work, it has been the object of the compiler to unite novelty with utility, and in all the detail of those designs, he has had a strict attention to their practicability, and while giving due regard to ornament, to maintain the greatest economy of labor. Most of those designs have been selected from the best examples of dwellings already finished; many of them, during their erection, being under the author's immediate superintendence. This experience has enabled him to make many improvements, which he conceives will render them more acceptable. There has been exhibited on each plate as much matter as it would admit of, some of the designs being replete with plans, sections and elevations, on a single plate; the whole accompanied with a scale of feet and inches. Among the important uses of this work, will be that of pointing out the various capacities for improvement, and the manifold methods of finish, in the detail of each building. The carpenter will be considerably benefitted by this production, as it will not only enable those who wish to build to express more clearly to him their views, but it will elicit new ones, of which they had previously no idea, and which the carpenter will be called upon to supply. The author begs leave to express his acknowledgments to his friends, for the liberal encouragement they have shown him in publishing this work in four monthly parts. For the patronage extended, he has made the best return in his power, by publishing this work at a price unprecedentedly low.

PLATE I.

A DWELLING WITH THREE ROOMS AND OTHER CONVENIENCES.

CONSTRUCTION.—The walls of the main body of the building are shown of stone; the middle part of the first story has rusticated corners; the corners of the wings have pilasters. The entrance door is at the end of the building; there is a door a few feet from the front door, which forms a lobby; the front entrance may be improved by adding a suitable portico. Objections may be made, by some persons, to the entrance door being at the end of the building;—but having it so, in the present arrangement, will decidedly make the house more comfortable. The centre window in the first story, may be made into a gibb window, which would give it the effect of an entrance in the centre of the front, and add to the comfort of the living room in warm weather;—by its opening clear down to the floor, would give free admission to air.

PLATE II.

A TWO STORY DWELLING, WITH AN ATTIC IN THE BACK BUILDING.

CONSTRUCTION.—All the outside walls are shown of nine inch brick,—the partition walls, of wood; the passage passing through the front building makes the whole of the rooms private. The double-light windows in the front building will admit an abundance of light, and by having the stairs out of the back entry, makes room to admit a window in the back parlor, corresponding with the one in the front. What

B

has been said of the windows in the first story, may be applied with equal exactness to the windows in the second story.   By having the attic to the back building, ample headway is given to ascend to the garret; the apex of the roof of the front building is nearer the back wall than the front, for the purpose of effecting a sufficient pitch for the back part of the roof.   The back wall of the main building is higher than the front wall, to give an entrance to the garret from the attic floor of the back building.   There can be an attic window in the back wall of the main building, corresponding in width to the double-light windows below. It is presumed that this dwelling possesses as many conveniences as could be well accomplished in so small a space, the front being only eighteen feet, and the whole depth fifty-eight feet.

PLATE III.

CONTAINS TWO PLANS; A SECTION AND AN ELEVATION, OF A DWELLING HOUSE OF SIX ROOMS, WITH VARIOUS CONVENIENCES.

ACCOMMODATION.—From the passage and stair-case there is a kitchen and wash-house; there is a cellar adjoining the kitchen.   If the cellar be sunk a sufficient depth to admit of a floor over it, there can be another room added, that will answer for a pantry or dairy.   The second story contains three good chambers, which are all private; also, a closet, which is lighted with a window from the passage.

CONSTRUCTION.—The whole of the walls may be framed of wood, with the exception of the wall for the chimnies, which should properly be entirely of brick or stone.   The window over the portico is a gibb window, which will permit persons to walk out on the portico.

PLATE IV.

IS A DESIGN FOR A HOUSE TWO STORIES HIGH, WITH AN ATTIC.

CONSTRUCTION.—All the outside walls are supposed to be of brick; the front wall to be faced with marble as high as the first floor; the front wall to be of sufficient thickness to receive inside shutters. The cornice may be of wood, but stone would be much better. The attic windows have sashes on the inside, which can be hung with lines, and slide up on the inside of the wall, or they may be hung with hinges, and fold as casement windows. The ornaments on the exterior of the windows are made of cast-iron, and painted the same color as the cornice, which has a very pleasing effect. There are two cellar-doors, which have a light of thick ground glass for the admission of light; the doors are hung with hinges at the top, and when open, have fastenings in the joists for the purpose of holding them in a horizontal position. The passages passing through the whole depth of this house, make all the rooms private. There is a window at the end of the passage in the back building, and should a door be required at the other end of the passage adjoining the back entry, it can be a sash door—which will make the passage sufficiently light. The doors dividing the parlors are made to slide in the partition. There is a wash-house adjoining the kitchen, where water is heated and conveyed to the bath-room above. There is a piazza in the second story, enclosed with venetian shutters, which will cause sufficient ventilation, so that the water-closet will not produce any unpleasant air that can be communicated to any part of the house. The section of the front indicates the heights of the stories. This design possesses a great many conveniences, and for a town residence, is a very desirable arrangement.

PLATE V

IS A DESIGN FOR A COTTAGE CONTAINING SEVEN ROOMS ON THE PRINCIPAL STORY, A BASEMENT, AND OTHER CONVENIENCES.

CONSTRUCTION.—The whole of the walls above the basement may be built of wood, with the exception of the passage walls where the chimneys are, which it is advisable should be entirely of brick or stone. The outside of the house may be boarded between the pilasters, the boards having a sinking where they join, for the purpose of imitating stone work with rusticated joints. The basement contains a kitchen, wash-house and other conveniences. The whole of the ground in the basement may be dug out, so as to use the whole of the surface the house occupies, or any part of it may be omitted, being removed as convenience may require. There is an area that surrounds the house, for the purpose of keeping the basement dry, and admitting light to the windows below the surface of the ground. The apex of the roof is sufficiently elevated to admit of two good rooms in the garret; there is a dormar window on each side of the roof; the roof is not hipped on all sides to the centre of the building, but there is a ridge fifteen feet long, running parallel to the sides of the building. The chimneys may be gathered into one group on each side of the passage, after they ascend the principal story, or they may come out on the roof separately, as taste may dictate. In the arrangement of this cottage, there are many conveniences, and the rooms differ in their dimensions, to suit the variety of uses for which they may be applied. This cottage is calculated for a genteel country residence, and to give it the best effect, it is necessary it should be erected on an elevated location.

PLATE VI.

A THREE STORY HOUSE WITH A BACK BUILDING.

CONSTRUCTION AND REMARKS.—Notwithstanding this dwelling has but twenty feet front, the interior arrangement is convenient and commodious. The passage in the front building occupies as little room as possible, to be convenient, the front part of it being only four feet, and increased in width to six feet, as far as the back parlor, to give room for the principal stairs.

The doors dividing the back and front parlors, slide into the partition, which is much better than when they are hung with hinges, as it avoids, when opened, their interfering with the furniture. The back parlor has a side light window, which is better adapted to the size of the room than having two windows, and makes a pleasing contrast with the windows in the front parlor. The front and back walls are of sufficient thickness to admit of inside shutters. The arrangements in the second story correspond with those of the first, with the exceptions of the addition of a dressing-room to the front chamber, and a single door that opens into the front and back rooms.

In the arrangements of the third story, the front and back chambers may have closets attached to them, similar to the plan of the second story of the design in Plate XII. There are two good garret rooms which are lighted with dormars. The back entry in the plan of the principal story is as small as it could be, to admit of a side light door; there is a china closet opposite the door, which is convenient to the breakfast room. The back stairs are near to the servants' apartments, and the entrance to the cellar is effected by a stairs directly under the back stairs. By this arrangement of the back stairs to separate the kitchen from the breakfast room, and having a door opening into the yard, any noise and unpleasantness in the culinary apartments will not incommode persons in the breakfast room. There is a wash house adjoining the kitchen, and the office in the rear of it is detached from the main part of the house, for the purpose of giving it access to the

C

open air. In the arrangement of the second story of the back building, it contains a bath room directly over the breakfast room, which can be supplied with hot water, by a very simple method now in use, which is that of a pipe communicating to a boiler fixed in the back of the kitchen fire place, or from the boiler in the wash house, as may be required. There is a store room over the wash house that is lighted with a window from the terrace. A door in the back chamber opens on the terrace that leads to the water closet. The terrace may be enclosed with trellis work, or venetian shutters, to give it sufficient privacy.

PLATE VII.

A ONE STORY COTTAGE, WITH A BASEMENT AND OTHER CONVENIENCES.

CONSTRUCTION AND REMARKS.—The whole of the walls in the basement should be built of stone or brick; the basement contains a kitchen, wash house, pantry, dairy, &c. The arrangement of the rooms corresponds with those in the principal story. The kitchen is under the breakfast room, and those other offices that require to be well lighted, are in the back part of the building. The ground on the back part of the house being lower than in the front part, will admit ample light.

The entrance to the basement is under the back steps, the steps forming a covering for the outside of the door. The principal floor contains six good rooms, a water closet and bath room. The whole of the walls may be framed of wood, with the exception of those where the chimneys are in the back part of the house, which would be best to be entirely of brick. The chimneys in the front part may be built against a wood partition, as indicated by its thickness on the plan. The area adjoining the water closet can be enclosed with venetian shutters, which will keep it quite private as well as properly ventilated. There is a piazza ten feet wide, that extends along the whole front, and returns on a part of the ends. By this arrangement it not only shields the parlor and dining room from the sun, *supposing them to have a southern exposure,* but relieves the building of the monotonous appearance arising from its cubical form, and adds greatly to the good effect of the whole structure. The apex of the roof is truncated, and a platform or observatory formed on it, and enclosed with ballustrading, which would be an agreeable retreat in mild weather. There is a lantern dome in the centre of the observatory, which admits light to the garret; a part of it opens, to enable persons to pass out; the means of access to the observatory is by a step ladder from the garret floor. This design is good in point of arrangement. The plan exhibits comfortable accommodation, and the whole of the rooms having immediate access to the passages, are thus made private. Although this house covers considerable surface, yet, from its compact, cubical form, the expense must necessarily be moderate in proportion to the accommodation afforded. The situation is supposed to be elevated, which will add materially to the general beauty of the whole edifice.

12

PLATE VIII.

A THREE STORY HOUSE WITH AN ATTIC AND BACK BUILDING.

CONSTRUCTION AND ACCOMMODATION.—The front building is twenty-five feet front, and forty-two feet deep. The principal story, including the back building, contains a portico, vestibule, two good parlors, a breakfast room, kitchen, wash house, &c. The whole of the rooms, offices, &c., have their dimensions affixed to them in the plans. There is a niche in the passage to receive a stove. There are niches in the circular part of the stairs, for the reception of figures; the back entry has a side light door, and opposite it is a china closet. The inside corner of the breakfast room is made circular, corresponding with the outside corner, which not only makes the room uniform, but admits the light to pass more directly into the passage. There is a staircase that ascends to the different stories in the back building,—and the entrance to the cellar is under the back stairs. There is a door under the back stairs that leads into the yard. The kitchen occupies the whole width of the back building, it being sixteen feet square. The corner of the kitchen is made circular to correspond with the other outside corner of the back building, which will give it a more pleasing effect than when made square. From the kitchen there is a door that leads into the wash house, and from the wash house a door leading into the yard. What has been said of the arrangement of the principal story, will apply equally to the second and third stories with these exceptions: the addition of a dressing room to the front chambers, and two closets to the front and back chambers. The bath room in the second story is directly over the wash house, and hot water can be easily communicated to the bath, from the wash house, or from a boiler fixed in the back of the kitchen fire-place. There are venetian shutters at the end of the passage, near the water closet, which, with the window in the water closet, will always keep those apartments properly ventilated. All the outside walls are supposed to be built of brick; the front wall being faced with stone as high as the floor of the principal story. The front windows have lintel cornices, supported with consols. The section of the front shows the different heights of the stories, the projection of the cornices, &c. The profile of the portico is shown below, drawn to the same scale.

By painting the front with some light color, the effect will be greatly improved, as the shadows of its numerous projecting members will be more minutely developed. There is an enlarged front, and profile view of the consols of the windows, drawn to the scale that accompanies them. The roof is intended to be covered with tin or zinc.

REMARKS.—The internal arrangement of this design is considered good, the passages extending through the whole depth of the building makes all the rooms private, and although the width of the front is small, the depth of the whole building is considerable, which renders ample accommodations for a large family.

PLATE IX.

A TWO STORY HOUSE WITH A BASEMENT AND OTHER CONVENIENCES.

The situation intended for this house is in an open lot; the ground rises gradually from the street, at the rate of about one foot in eight, and the house intended to be placed back from it about forty feet; the yard, stables, &c., arranged at the back of the house. The front elevation to stand towards the west, the entrance door being on the north side; the flanks of the lot adjoining the house, to be enclosed with a wall, and the front with iron railing.

D

CONSTRUCTION AND ARRANGEMENT.—The basement contains a kitchen, pantry, wine cellar and servants' room; the latter may be used as a man's bed room. The entrance to the basement is by the steps in the area on the south side. The stairs in the entry ascend to the principal story, and land under the principal stairs. There are two distinct circular openings outside the front wall, for the admission of light to the front windows of the basement. The principal story contains a drawing room, parlor and breakfast room or library.

The outside walls are built of stone. The partition wall, running parallel to the front wall, to be built of nine inch brick, which supports the joist. All the other partition walls may be built of wood. The doors dividing the drawing room and parlor are made to slide into the partition. There are niches formed in the circular walls of the stair case for the reception of statues. The end walls are battened on the inside, to avoid any angles in the walls caused by the projections of the chimney breasts in the room. This being done, it not only makes the walls straight but keeps them much drier. The arrangement of the rooms in the second story corresponds with those on the principal story; the small room over the front entry is lighted by a window in the back part of the house, and may be converted into a water closet or bath room as may be required. There are two good garret rooms that are lighted by the segment windows in the ends of the house. The flues of the chimneys are gathered in, over the segment windows to form one group, as indicated by the end elevation. There is an elliptical dome in the roof, corresponding with the plan of the stairs, that admits ample light to the stairs, passages, &c., below. There is a niche in the front between the windows, also a niche in the centre of the end elevation, where figures may be placed. The whole of the exterior walls are supposed to be built of dressed stone, or made to imitate it, by being roughcast.

REMARKS.—Considering the size of this house, there is a great deal of comfort in the design, and much economy of both room and labor, are obtained in the general arrangement. Although the accommodations are rather limited, they were considered amply sufficient for a gentleman without any family, for which it was designed. The effect of the exterior is conceived to be good. The architraves around the windows, the angular pilasters, together with the denticulated cornice and ornamental chimney tops, are in keeping with each other, and form an agreeable whole.

PLATE X.

A TWO STORY HOUSE, WITH A BASEMENT AND BACK BUILDING.

CONSTRUCTION AND ACCOMMODATION.—Plate X. contains a plan of the basement and principal stories, and Plate XI. the elevation of a dwelling with twelve rooms and other conveniences.   The front of the basement wall is faced with stone as high as the floor of the principal story; the joints of the stones are sunk or rusticated.   The best stairs ascending to the principal story are near the front door; the door leading to the back part of the basement is under the stairs, and it has side lights which give light to the passage from the front door.   The front room may be used as an office or visiting room, and has two doors—the inside door being quite private from the outside one.   The back stairs are in the back entry, it being the most central and convenient.   The kitchen is spacious and commodious; from the kitchen a door opens into the yard, and near to the kitchen door is the entrance to the wash house.   The entrance to the back offices is protected from the weather by the projection of the piazza above.   The arrangement of the rooms in the principal story corresponds with those on the basement story; the principal stairs are at the extreme end of the passage, and have niches in the circular part of the wall, to contain figures with lamps to light the stairs at night.   The doors dividing the drawing room and parlor are sliding doors.   The means of access to the bath room and water closet is by a door in the back bed-room which opens on a piazza; the piazza being enclosed with venetian shutters which keep those offices quite private, as well as properly ventilated.   What has been said of the arrangement of the rooms of the principal story, *with the exception of the back offices*, may be applied with equal exactness to the third story; that part of the back building occupied by the bath room and water closet does not extend higher than the principal story.   The garret contains three good rooms, two being on the front and one on the back of the garret floor.

Plate XI. contains an elevation and section of the plans of Plate X.; the windows of the principal story extend to the floor and have ornamental guards affixed to them on the outside.   The gable walls are elevated above the roof as a protection from adjacent fires.

PLATES XI., XII.

CONTAIN AN ELEVATION AND TWO PLANS OF A THREE STORY HOUSE WITH A BACK BUILDING.

ACCOMMODATIONS.—The principal floor shows a portico, and an entrance hall; a door in the entrance hall opens into an anti-room; the anti-room has a private door in the passage. The principal stairs are open to the passage. There are two Corinthian columns on a direct line with the passage, which support the landing of the stairs above; opposite to the stairs are the entrances to the drawing room and parlor; those rooms are each twenty-two by sixteen feet, and fourteen feet high, the large doors in them are made to slide. From the principal stairs a door leads into the pantry, and from the pantry a private door leads into the dining room, also a door into the back entry; the back stairs are in the entry; from the entry a door opens into the breakfast room; the breakfast room is made private by the passage leading into the kitchen; from the kitchen a door opens into the wash house, also a door into the yard. The front building of the second story contains a principal chamber and back chamber, each of them have closets attached to them; there is a ladies' chamber in the front part. Where economy is an object, the principal stairs need not be continued farther than the second story, the back stairs answering all purposes above the second story; there is a dome corresponding with the form of the stairs which admits light to the passages, &c. below; a passage extends through the back building, communicating to the bath room and water closet; the water closet is supposed to be attached to the end of the passage.

CONSTRUCTION.—All the outside walls are supposed to be of brick, also the centre wall of the front building, and the division wall of the breakfast room and kitchen; the front wall is faced with marble as high as the floor of the principal story; the portico, window heads and cornices, are of the same material, or in imitation of it. The pitch of the roof is adapted to be covered with zinc or tin, the front cornice having a ballustraded parapet. If garrets should be required, it will be necessary to elevate the pitch of the roof, and if light cannot be obtained from the ends of the house, dormars could be so constructed that on viewing the front, the parapets would conceal their being seen. The section of the front indicates the height of the stories.

REMARKS.—This design possesses a great deal of accommodation as well as beauty, and they are obtained with the least possible width of front, for a house that has rooms on each side of the front entrance. The principal stairs are easy of access, and when viewed from the passage through the intercolumniation, the effect is good. If the wall in which the chimneys are in the front building does not adjoin a house, light procured from a double light window in the second story, and two small dressing rooms substituted for the closets shown on the plan, would add materially to the conveniences of both chambers.

PLATE XIII.

A DESIGN FOR A THREE STORY HOUSE IN THE GRECIAN STYLE, ADAPTED FOR A LARGE FAMILY.

The general features and arrangement of this design are taken from a house at the intersection of Locust and Thirteenth streets, Philadelphia, where it was built a few years since by John Hare Powell, Esq.

Construction and Accommodation.—The kitchen is in the basement, directly under the dining room. The stairs descending to the basement are under the winding stairs, shown in the plan of the principal story. There is a vault under the front portico, the wall of which makes a good foundation for the portico and steps. There is a well under the drawing room of greater depth than the vault, which is intended to keep the whole of the cellar, &c., dry. The principal story contains a portico and an entrance hall; from the hall there is a door on the right that opens into an anti-room, and a private door on the left that opens into the principal staircase; opposite to the entrance door, there is a door that opens into the vestibule; the vestibule has a private door that leads into the anti-room, which may be used as a business or visiting room. There is also a corresponding door that leads into the principal stairs; there are three other doors in the vestibule; one opening into the saloon room, one into the drawing room, and one into the dining room. There are three windows in the saloon room, one on each side of the fire place, in the form of French casements, extending down to the floor, which enables persons to pass out into a portico which communicates to the back of the house; the centre window is immediately over the fire place, the bottom of the window being level with the top of the mantel-piece; the flue of the fire place is carried up in the pier of the windows as shown on the plan. The doors on each side of the saloon slide into the partitions, and when open produce an enfilade of three rooms; there are also sliding doors which unite the anti-room with the drawing room. The drawing room and dining room have bay windows; and the walls forming the bay windows extend from the basement to

E

the roof.   From the anti-room a door communicates to the green house; a private door, also, leads into the gardener's room; the gardener's room has an apparatus for heating the green house, and the same apparatus may be made to extend heat to all parts of the dwelling.   The soil pipe from the water closet, passes down the corner of the gardener's room, and communicates to a sewer.   From the principal stairs a door leads into the entry of the butler's pantry and servants' room.   There is a corresponding door to a closet on the other side, and between those doors there is a recess in the wall that is intended for a dumb waiter to communicate from the basement to the principal story to facilitate the serving up of dinner, &c., from the kitchen to the dining room.   The principal stairs ascend to the platform with a centre flight of steps, and two return flights from the platform ascend to the second story; there are two niches on the platform for the reception of figures standing on pedestals and holding lamps for the purpose of giving light at night to the stairs, entries, &c.

The second story contains a summer sitting room which is also the principal entry to all the rooms.   The general arrangement of the rooms and their dimensions correspond with those on the principal floor.   From the breakfast room a door opens and steps descend to the water closet and bath room.   The bath room may have a boiler fixed in it for heating water, or the bath may be supplied with hot water from the heating apparatus in the gardener's room below.   The rooms on the third story are similar to the rooms on the second floor. All the outside walls are supposed to be built of stone, or made to imitate it by being roughcasting.

P L A T E   X I V.

Contains the front elevation and section of the plans of Plate XIII., the windows in the second story are near to the floor.   The attic windows are made to slide up into the wall, as indicated by the section.

19

PLATE XV.

Shows the back elevation of Plates XIII. and XIV. The kitchen receives light by an area outside the windows, whose depth is level with the kitchen floor. The windows in the drawing room and dining room extend to the floor; also the two side windows in the saloon, and the windows of the centre chambers over them. The freize of the cornice is not continued on the back part of the house, but terminates on the angular pilasters, for the purpose of having the windows in the third story higher than those of the front.

REMARKS.—The interior arrangement of this design is considered to be good, and the exterior, simple and harmonious. Owing to the cubical form of the building, the expense must consequently be moderate in proportion to the spacious rooms and conveniences afforded. Objections may be made by some persons to the kitchen being in the basement, but as the principal floor is considerably elevated, it is presumed the kitchen will be sufficiently ventilated. The servants' room may be converted into a kitchen, and all the necessary offices attached to it, outside the steps. There may be steps in the area leading down to the basement kitchen, which would add materially to its convenience. The side lights of the door dividing the hall and vestibule, should have ground glass, or if stained glass were used, it would not only make the vestible more private, but greatly improve the effect in both apartments. The beauty of the drawing room may be enhanced by the introduction of a window on each side of the fire place, so that the green house may be viewed from the drawing room. Those windows could be made flush with the wall so as not to interfere with the furnishing of the room. The two principal chambers may have dressing rooms appended to them by reducing their lengths, and windows placed at the ends of the house to light them. By having a passage dividing the front and back rooms in the third story, that part over the summer sitting room may be made a private room.

PLATE XVI.

A THREE STORY HOUSE WITH A BACK BUILDING, SUITABLE FOR A LARGE FAMILY.

ACCOMMODATION.—In the ground plan from the portico the front door opens into an octagonal vestibule, the openings for the side lights of the front and passage doors occupy four sides of the vestibule, those openings have sashes on both sides, the sashes towards the vestibule may have stained glass in them, and a figure to be placed in each of those openings holding a lamp to give light to the vestibule at night. The four rooms in the front building have a door that opens into the principal passage. The parlor and breakfast room have a door that leads into the private passage. In the drawing room there are two Corinthian columns, one on each side of the sliding doors, supporting a projecting entablature; on the other side of the doors in the dining room, there are two corresponding columns, *in antæ*, the entablature of which is not broken, but follows the line of the room. The circular part of the wall of the principal stairs has niches formed in it to contain vases, or any other appropriate ornament; there is a window under the stairs, which, with the side lights of the front door, &c., gives ample light to the passage. On the entrance to the private passage there are two columns in antæ, and opposite them there is a niche for the reception of a figure, holding a lamp to light the passages at night; there is a window shown on the end of the house, to give light to the private passage, but if light cannot be procured in this direction, the breakfast room may have a sash door opposite to the window, to give borrowed light to the passage, if required. The private passage leads into the back entry; the back entry has a side light door, and opposite to this door is the stair case that communicates to the different stories in the back building. The entrance to the cellar is under these stairs. There is a door that opens into a light closet, and a door that leads into the kitchen; from the kitchen there is a door that opens into the wash house, and from the wash house a door leads into the yard. The arrangement of the rooms in the second and third stories may correspond with those on the principal story, with the addition to the principal chamber of a dressing room over the vestibule; over the wash house would be the bath room, and next to it the water closet, which may be projected from the floor of the bath room; the soil pipe from the water closet may be formed by a division in the wall of the wash house, or a metallic tube may pass down on the outside of the wall, and communicate to a sewer.   If it should be desired to have the water closet private from the bath room, it may be effected by drawing the flues in the wall nearer the windows, to give room for a passage to enable persons to pass into the water closet without entering the bath room.   The section indicates the heights of the stories.

REMARKS.—The internal arrangement of this design is excellent, the rooms being spacious, and their high style of finish produces a magnificent effect.   The form of the hall or vestibule is good; the passages with their columns, niches, &c. harmonize with the general features of the house.   The front elevation with its portico, side light windows and projecting curves, produces a varied and an agreeable front.

P L A T E   X V I I .

A COTTAGE WITH FIVE ROOMS, FOR A SMALL FAMILY.

ACCOMMODATION.—The entrance hall or porch, is lighted with a side light door; from the hall a door opens into the living room, also a door leads into the parlor; from the living room there are two doors—one opens into the kitchen, and the other leads into a bed room; there is a door in the parlor that opens into another bed room; there is a door in the kitchen that opens into the back yard.   On each side of the hall there is a door that leads out on the veranda, and at each end of the veranda there is a door that opens into the back yard.

F

CONSTRUCTION.—The whole of the walls are intended to be built of wood, the chimneys alone to be built of brick; the colonnade or veranda has twin columns to support the roof. The dimensions of those columns being small, they may be made of cast-iron; the roof of the veranda may be covered with canvas or thin boards, and painted. The windows may be hung with lines, according to the usual method of making windows, but in this design they are shown as casements, it being most becoming for the cottage style. This design is well calculated for being executed at a very moderate expense. As all the masonry required would be for the chimneys and the foundations of the walls, there is no space taken up for passages; yet the rooms are sufficiently private, as the living room and parlor can be entered from the hall separately; the back of the house can be approached on each flank of the veranda, by the two doors shown at the ends of the veranda.

PLATE XVIII.

A VILLA, ADAPTED FOR AN ELEVATED SITUATION.

The situation of this house is supposed to be on the face of a bank, sloping towards the back part. The area before the entrance door is raised nearly to a level with the principal floor on that side, while on the back part of the house the kitchen floor appears entirely above ground.

ACCOMMODATION.—The principal story shows the main entrance; the hall is lighted by the circular transom over the door. There is a closet on each side of the front door; one of them is divided, and a part of it attached to the library—the other part is intended for holding hats, umbrellas, &c. The closet on the other side may be attached to the parlor similar to that of the library, or it may be made a fire-proof closet if required. The vestibule is lighted by a lantern dome in the roof; there is a large semi-elliptical recess opposite the front door, and on one side of it is the stairs descending to the basement, and on the other side is the entrance to the stairs ascending to the second story. From the vestibule there are doors leading into all the rooms; the drawing room and parlor are connected by sliding doors; there is a door in the drawing room which leads into the breakfast room, and from the breakfast room there is a door that opens into the dining room. The bath room, water closet, and other necessary offices, are supposed to be in the basement story. It is supposed there are seven rooms in the second story, three being over the dining room and parlor, one over the hall, and one over each of the other rooms. There is an opening in the floor of the second story to admit light from the dome to the vestibule, and this opening is surrounded with ballustrading. The ceiling of the vestibule is groined up to this opening, which conceals that part of the stairs which comes in the vestibule. The section indicates the heights of the stories; all the main walls are supposed to be built of stone, that of the basement outside walls of dressed rusticated stone work, and the upper stories of rubble stone work, and roughcasted; or, where economy is not an object, the whole of the outside walls above the basement may be built of dressed stone.

REMARKS.—This villa is replete with comfort, convenience, and even luxury; the walls are shown of considerable thickness, which would tend to keep the house warmer in cold weather, and more cool than thin walls during the summer season. The elevations on all sides are simple, and have a dignified appearance, their surfaces being broken with the centre projections and angular pilasters, creates a variety of shadow and greatly adds to the general good effect of the whole structure. The hall may be enlarged by dispensing with the closets, but as the front door has no side lights, the space those closets occupy can be conveniently disposed of.

PLATE XIX.

A PORTABLE COTTAGE, FOR THE USE OF NEW SETTLERS AND OTHERS.

The principal object of this portable cottage is to supply persons with comfortable and secure lodgings, immediately on their arrival at a new settlement. The secondary uses of this cottage are, that it may be packed in a small space, and carried in ships making long voyages, for the purpose of being set up on shore wherever any stay is made, either for the benefit of invalids or for the use of scientific persons. Its weight would not exceed a ton, and might therefore be easily drawn with one horse. Where public works are going on in any remote district, one of these cottages would form a very convenient dwelling for the overseer, and being put on wheels, might be moved forward as the work progressed. This cottage would be found a source of great comfort to persons who frequently have occasion to move their location, as it could be put up by two men in two hours, and taken down again in even less time. The accommodation of this dwelling is limited to two rooms, each twelve feet by twelve feet, and eight feet high. One of them may have a stove, as shown at d, the pipe of which may be carried up within a piece of sheet iron fastened on the tarpawling, which serves as a temporary roof; the whole of the stove is supposed to be of wrought iron, for lightness.

CONSTRUCTION.—The foundations of this structure consist of four sleepers $e, e, e, e,$ each thirteen feet long and six inches deep, by three inches thick; on these are placed grooved bottom plates $f, f, f, f,$ forming the foundations of the flooring, and the outside walls; those plates are formed of pieces six inches wide, and three inches thick, laid flatwise and grooved along the upper side to receive the bottom rails of the panelled frames which form the walls of the cottage. These plates are let into the sleepers in the manner shown by fig. A and D. (to a scale of an inch and a half to a foot,) fig. A shows the bottom plate with the corner post let into it, in which is fixed a screw nut, for being taken hold of by a screw bolt which passes through the bottom plate—so that by means of a wrench it can be screwed perfectly tight. The corner posts are eight feet long and four inches by four inches on the sides; there are seven intermediate posts in each side partition, each of which is three inches by three inches on the sides. There are five joists, each six by two inches, which are fitted on the sleepers and the bottom plate, as indicated at A and D. The posts are grooved on the sides, and so are the top and bottom plates, for the purpose of receiving in the grooves the end of the panelled frames. When the cottage is being put together, the panelled frames fig. C, (to a scale of an inch and a half to a foot) are put in between the grooved posts; two of these pannels are in part glazed, and hinged to the corner posts, thus forming at once all the doors and windows required. On the top plate are placed the rafters, seven feet long, four inches wide, and an inch and a half thick, which are let into a ridge piece at the top, and into the wall plate at the bottom. A purlin is placed across the rafters on each side, halved into them, and flush at the top. The flooring is formed of inch pine boards, and may be tongued and grooved. The construction of the frames will be understood by fig. C. *i.* is the corner post rabbeted for the door; *g.* one of the middle posts; *h. h. h.* the stiles, and *m. m.* the panels of one of the frames. Fig. B shows one of the middle posts, with the side and partition frames grooved into it. The roof is generally completed by a tarpawling, which is thrown over the rafters, and having strings on the under side, is made tight by them to the rafters, while it is kept close down at the eaves by lines which are sewed along the margins of the canvas, and tied tight at the angles. In damp situations the sleepers may be elevated on short posts or stones, so as to raise the floor from the surface, in order to keep it dry.

R E M A R K S.—This cottage is considered a very perfect one of the kind—every part of it being made exactly of the same dimensions: that is—all the panels, posts and plates, being respectively of the same length, breadth and thickness; no mistake or loss of time can occur in putting them together. Another important consideration in the construction is, that not a single nail is used either in the carpentry of the separate parts, or in putting those parts together to form the cottage.

All the frame work composing the sides of the cottage being grooved and tongued, the weather is most effectually kept out, and at the same time this mode of construction allows the work to shrink and swell according to the changes of the atmosphere or the season, without deranging any of its parts. When a permanent situation is fixed on, the cottage may be covered with shingles or such other material as may be most readily obtained.

G

PLATE XX.

A DESIGN FOR A FOUR STORY WAREHOUSE.

The plan is twenty-five feet front by sixty feet deep. The side walls are fourteen inches thick; the front and back walls are eighteen inches thick in the first and second stories; fourteen inches in the third story, and nine inches in the fourth story. The front piers and entablature of the first story are supposed to be of granite. The section of the front indicates the heights of the stories. Fig. A shows a section of the granite front to a scale of three-eighths of an inch to a foot.

PLATE XXI.

A VILLA TWO STORIES HIGH, WITH A BASEMENT, &c.

ACCOMMODATION AND CONSTRUCTION.—The basement is supposed to contain a kitchen, under the library. The wing under the library is used as a scullery and wash house, and the wing under the drawing room is a man's bed room; that part of the basement under the drawing room is subdivided into a butler's pantry, larder, &c. The centre part under the dining room may be arranged into compartments for the various purposes which a house of this kind requires, viz: a wine cellar store-room, pantry, &c. From the basement the stairs ascend to the hall in the principal story. The principal story contains a porch, which has openings with circular heads in its ends; from the porch the front doors open into the hall, and on each end of the hall there is a door—one which opens into the drawing room, and another that opens into the library. The recesses formed by the angular pilasters in the library are sufficiently wide to receive folding doors, when opened, if they should be required, to separate the wing from the main part of the library, so as to form two distinct rooms. The entrance to the dining room is from the hall under the stairs; there are steps outside the dining room window which admit persons to pass out into the garden. The second story contains three principal bed rooms, the wing over the library being used as a dressing room, with a bath in it; the means by which this bath is supplied with hot and cold water, is similar to the one already referred to in a former part of this work, and which may be understood by the following description:—At any time a hot or cold bath may be obtained, without the assistance of servants, by the use of the following means: there is a cold water cistern under the roof, and a hot water cistern at the back of the kitchen fire-place; in this last cistern there is a coil of leaden pipe, one end of the pipe communicating with the cold water cistern above, and the other with the bath. By turning a cock in the bath room the water descends from the cistern under the roof, is heated in passing through the coil of pipes behind the kitchen fire, and ascends, by the pressure of the atmosphere on the cistern, to the bath. Another cock and pipe leading directly from the cistern, admit cold water to the bath, which tempers it at pleasure; and a third pipe serves to carry off the water when done with. There are two small rooms taken from the front part of the rooms over the drawing room and library; one of which may be used as a bed room, and the other as a water closet. The wing over the drawing room may be used as a nursery or dressing room, attached to the bed room. There may be two garret rooms formed in the main part of the building, and lighted with dormars from the back part of the house. The wings do not extend higher than the eaves of the main building, as indicated by the elevation. The section shows the heights of the stories. The walls are of stone or brick, eighteen inches thick, to the height of the principal floor, above which they are about fourteen inches in thickness; exteriorly, they are supposed to be covered with roughcast, and the courses and sizes of the stones marked by lines. The windows have architraves around them on the outside.

REMARKS.—Considering the size of this villa, its completeness, and the extent of its accommodations, it is a design well worthy of imitation. The interior arrangement is judiciously planned. No room is lost in passages, not an inch of space is wasted on any floor, and every comfort and accommodation is included that can be desired in a house of its dimensions. The varied form of the plan produces an irregularity in the general elevation, which materially adds to the good effect of the exterior.

PLATE XXII.

A VILLA TWO STORIES HIGH, ADAPTED TO A SMALL FAMILY.

ACCOMMODATION.—The principal floor, the main entrance to the house, is by a flight of steps to the porch. There is another flight of steps on the back, giving access to the garden. A smaller flight of steps leads from the kitchen passage to the yard. From the porch the front door opens into a vestibule and principal stairs. On one side of the vestibule, a door opens into a lobby which is the entrance to the morning room, drawing room and library. The flue of the fire-place in the morning room is carried over the door of the drawing room. There are folding doors which separate the drawing room from the library. From the vestibule a door opens into the dining room; in the dining room there are French windows, which enable persons to pass out on the steps that lead into the garden. There is a door which leads from the vestibule into the private passage that communicates with the kitchen and other apartments. There is a back stairs in the private passage which ascends to the second story, in the manner shown on the plan of the second story; underneath those stairs there is a stairs which descends to the cellar. From the private passage there is a door that opens into the man's bed room; also a door which leads into the kitchen. From the kitchen there are two doors—one of which opens into the scullery, and the other into the larder. The second story contains one principal chamber and three smaller ones; also, a bath room and water closet. On the landing of the principal stairs a French window opens out on the gallery. On each end of the gallery there is a circular head opening that gives access to the terraces. In the principal chamber there is a door that opens into the back gallery; there is a window on each side of this door which admits light to the chamber. The principal end elevation is shown; also, the front elevation. The section shows the heights of the stories.

REMARKS.—This design has been considered in good taste. Its exterior is highly architectural, and every part of the interior is arranged for comfortable and elegant enjoyment. The accommodation may be greatly increased, and at a very moderate expense, viz: by elevating the principal floor a few feet, a basement may be formed which would exclude the kitchen and other offices from the principal floor, and make room for other apartments. The present arrangement will suit some situations better than others, as well as please those persons who like to have the culinary apartments above the surface of the ground.

PLATE XXIII.

A SUBURBAN TAVERN AND PLEASURE HOUSE.

ACCOMMODATION.—The ground floor shows a bar-room and sitting room on one side of the passage, and a front and back parlor on the other side of the passage. The kitchen is in the back building, which is one story high, with an attic; the attic is approached from the platform of the front stairs. Around the main building is a piazza, elevated one step above the surface of the ground. It is intended that the cellar

H

be confined to one side of the passage under the bar and sitting rooms, the door to the cellar being near the outside kitchen door. The arrangement of the rooms in the second story is supposed to correspond with those on the first floor; both the first and second floors have French windows—the sills of them being nearly level with the floor enable persons to pass out on the piazzas. The windows have Venitian shutters to them, by which the inmates of the house can keep those rooms, which are intended for their own use, quite private, and also admit fresh air at all times.

CONSTRUCTION.—By the thickness of the walls shown on the plan, they are supposed to be built of stone, the outside walls being sixteen inches thick, and the two partition walls fourteen inches thick. The floors of the piazzas are formed by the joists of the rooms projecting from the walls. The rafters of the roof extend outside the walls, sufficiently far for the roof of the piazzas below. The piazzas may have seats for the accommodation of those who wish to sit in the open air.

PLATE XXIV.

DESIGN FOR A DOUBLE HOUSE WITH A BACK BUILDING.

ACCOMMODATION.—The ground floor contains a portico, which extends along the whole front. The passage is eight feet wide; there is a sitting room in the front part of the house; from the sitting room there is a door that opens into the dining room; the back staircase is in the main building, a partition only separating the back from the front stairs. There are five steps that ascend from the wide winder of the front stairs to the landing of the back stairs on the second story. In the back building there is a pantry, and in it there are two closets.   From the pantry there is a door that opens into the kitchen, and from the kitchen there is a door that leads into the yard; the wash house and other necessary offices are supposed to be attached to the rear of the kitchen.   The principal floor is supposed to be the second story which contains the parlor and drawing room.   The arrangement of the rooms in the second story corresponds with those on the ground floor.   The third story contains two good bed rooms in the main building, and over them there are two garret rooms, which may be lighted from the end wall, if light can be obtained from this direction, or they may be lighted with sky lights or dormars.   The back building contains two chambers—one being in the second story and one in the attic.

CONSTRUCTION.—All the main walls of the houses are supposed to be built of brick—the front and back walls being of sufficient thickness to admit of inside shutters on the first and second stories.   The front windows in the second story have stone lintels, supported by consols; the windows extend to the floor, which admit of persons passing out on the portico.   The windows in the third story have plain stone lintels.   The roof is supposed to be covered with tin or zinc.   The section indicates the heights of the stories, the profile of the portico, consols, cornice, &c.

REMARKS.—Considering the size of each of those houses, the front being only twenty-nine feet and the depth forty-one feet, exclusive of the back building.   They possess sufficient accommodations for a large family, as well as a considerable degree of elegance on the exterior.   The front wall would look best if it were of worked stone as high as the second floor, and the remainder of the front above if of brick, to be painted a light color.   If the back building were extended, and the present kitchen used as a breakfast room, the first floor may be used for the principal rooms and those of the second story as chambers.

DRAWING PLANS AND ELEVATIONS.

THE following is offered as an addenda to the foregoing designs, for the use of the student in drawing plans and elevations of houses. The practitioner will first lay down the scale that he intends to work by; in doing this he may divide it decimally or into twelfths, but remember to adhere rigidly to it, for the dimensions of every part and item of your drawing. In drawing a plan he will suppose the building to be raised just above the floors; and the walls being level, he will proceed to resemble it as near as possible by lines drawn with a lead pencil. After laying down the exterior dimensions of the building, he will proceed to place down the thickness of the walls, and the partitions, doors, windows, &c. in their proper places. The plan of all the steps of the stairs should be laid down to show where they will land in the next story. When the plan is entirely drawn with a lead pencil, proceed to complete it with a drawing pen and India ink, carefully stopping the lines at the different openings, angles, &c. This being done, clean it off with a piece of India-rubber, and it will be ready for coloring, if required.

What has been said respecting the mode of proceeding in drawing plans, will apply with equal exactness in the drawing of elevations. In shading an elevation, the operator will conceive the light to come from one direction only, and that too in parallel rays.

The sun, the principal source of light, is so far distant from the earth, that the rays of light coming from it may be regarded as parallel. As in the shading of elevations, it is only necessary to find the shades and shadows as they appear in nature; the rays of light should be parallel with each other. In architectural drawings, it is customary to suppose the source of light on the left of the object; but this should be subject to exceptions, as the position of some houses prevents the sun's rays from coming in that direction, it would be unnatural to follow such a precedent. The rays of light should have such a direction that their horizontal and vertical projections will make angles of 45° with the ground line, or, *in other words, a right mitre.* This or any other angle can be obtained by the protractor that generally accompanies a case of instruments. When an angle of 45° is determined on for the direction of the light, it is plain that the rays will be parallel to the diagonal of a cube, whose faces are parallel and perpendicular to the planes of projection; and as the diagonal of a cube makes an angle of 35° 16′ with the plane of either of its faces, it follows that any ray of light will make an angle of 35° 16′ with the planes of projection, when both the projections of the cube make angles of 45° with the ground line. By following the above rules for shading elevations, the projections of their different members can always be obtained, viz: by measuring the shadows cast on their surfaces.

FINIS.

Plate 1.

Section

Front Elevation.

9.6

10.0

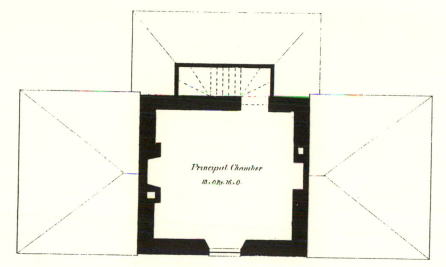

Principal Chamber
13.0 By 16.0.

Plan of 2ⁿᵈ Story

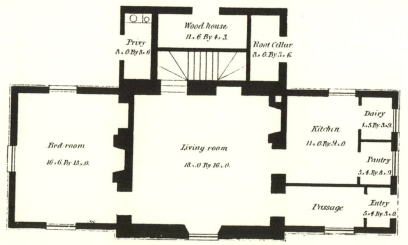

Privy
8.0 By 3.6

Wood house
11.6 By 4.3.

Root Cellar
8.0 By 3.6.

Bed-room
16.6 By 13.0.

Living room
13.0 By 16.0.

Kitchen
11.0 By 9.0.

Dairy
4.5 By 3.9.

Pantry
5.4 By 8.9.

Passage

Entry
5.4 By 3.0

Plan of principal Story 49 feet 6 in Front.

Scale   10   20   30   40   50 Feet.

Lith. by E. Weber & Co. Balt.

Plate 2.

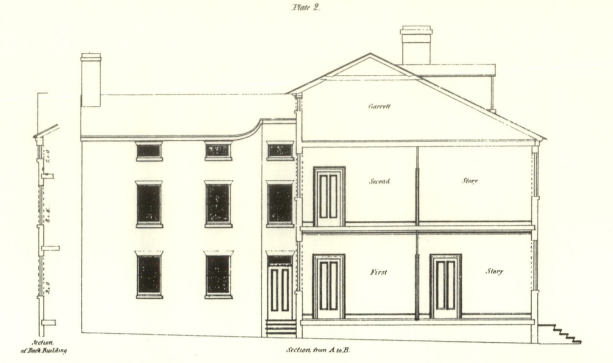

Section of Back Building

Section from A to B.

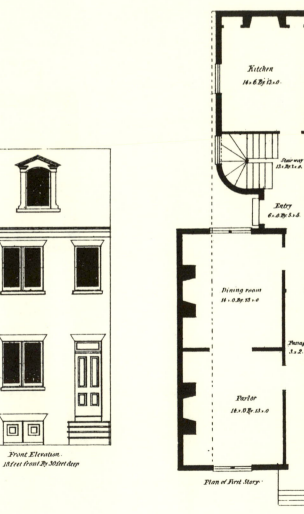

Garrett

Second   Story

First   Story

Back Chamber
14 . 6 By 13 . 0

Chamber
14 . 0 By 13 . 0

3 . 2

Principal Chamber
16 . 6 By 14 . 0

Plan of 2nd Story

Front Elevation.
18 feet front By 30 feet deep

Kitchen
14 . 6 By 13 . 0

Stair way
13 . 0 By 8 . 0

Entry
6 . 0 By 5 . 6

Dining room
14 . 0 By 13 . 0

Passage
3 . 2

Parlor
14 . 0 By 13 . 0

Whole depth 38 Feet deep

Plan of First Story

Scale   10   20   30   40   50 *Feet.*

of

I. Mohr Fecit.

Plate 3.

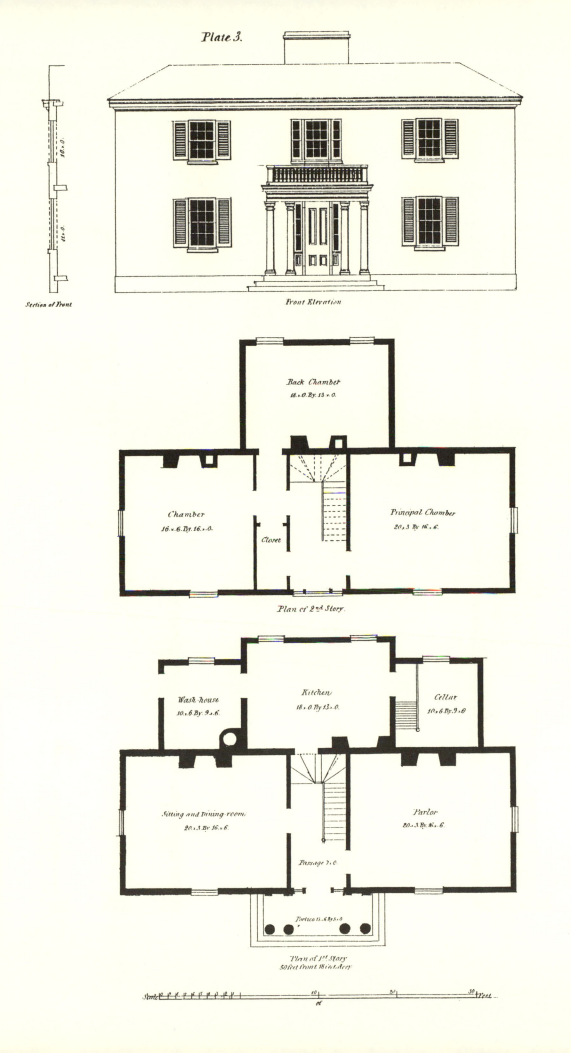

Section of Front

Front Elevation

Back Chamber
18 x 0. By 13 x 0.

Chamber
16 x 6. By 16 x 0.

Closet

Principal Chamber
20, 3 By 16', 6.

Plan of 2nd Story.

Wash house
10 x 6 By 9 x 6.

Kitchen
18 x 0 By 13 x 0.

Cellar
10 x 6 By 9 x 0

Sitting and Dining room.
20, 3 By 16 x 6.

Parlor
20, 3 By 16, 6.

Passage 7 x 0.

Portico 15 x 6 By 5 x 0

Plan of 1st Story.
50 feet Front 18 feet deep

Scale   10   20   30   Feet

Plate 4

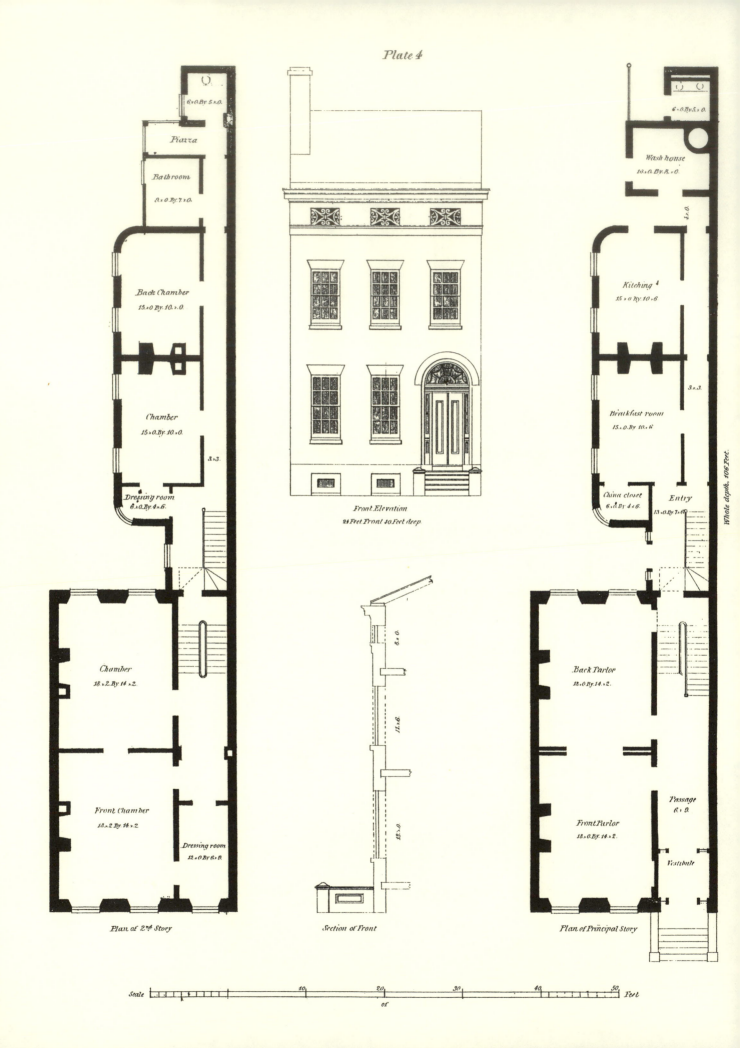

Piazza

Bathroom
0 x 0 By 7 x 0.

Back Chamber
15 x 0 By 10 x 0.

Chamber
15 x 0 By 10 x 0.

3 x 3.

Dressing room
6 x 0 By 4 x 6.

Front Elevation
24 Feet Front 40 Feet deep.

Wash house
10 x 0 By 8 x 0.

4 x 0.

Kitching
15 x 0 By 10 x 6.

3 x 3.

Breakfast room
15 x 0 By 10 x 6.

China closet
6 x 0 By 4 x 6.

Entry
13 x 0 By 7 x 6.

Chamber
18 x 2 By 14 x 2.

Back Parlor
18 x 0 By 14 x 2.

Front Chamber
18 x 2 By 14 x 2.

Dressing room
12 x 0 By 6 x 9.

Passage
6 x 9.

Front Parlor
18 x 0 By 14 x 2.

Vestibule

Plan of 2nd Story

Section of Front

Plan of Principal Story

Whole depth, 106 Feet.

Scale   10   20   30   40   50   Feet

Plate 5.

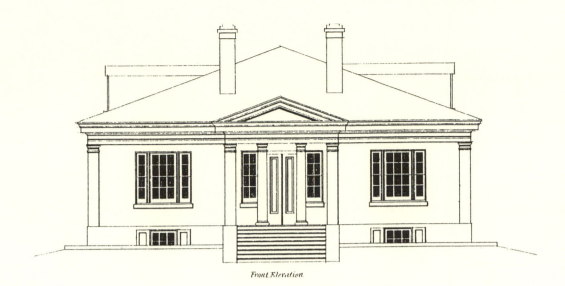

Front Elevation.

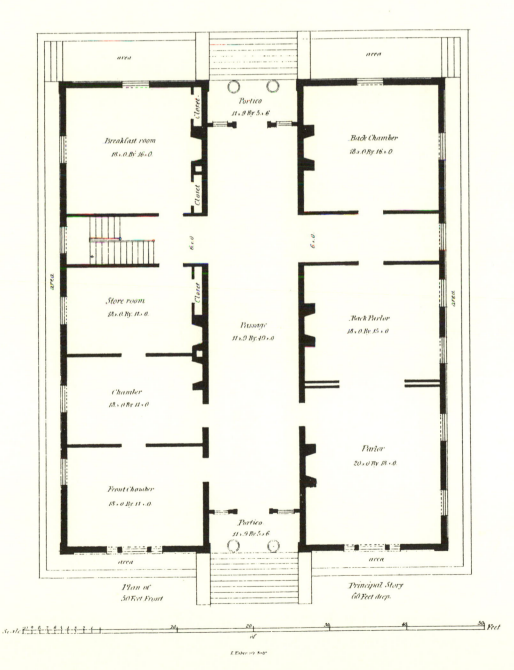

area   area

Portico
11 . 9 By 5 . 6

Closet

Breakfast room   Back Chamber
18 . 0 By 16 . 0.   18 . 0 By 16 . 0

Closet

area   6 . 0   6 . 0   area

Store room   Closet   Back Parlor
13 . 0 By 11 . 0.   18 . 0 By 15 . 0

                              Passage
Chamber   11 . 9 By 49 . 0
13 . 0 By 11 . 0

                                            Parlor
                                            20 . 0 By 18 . 0

Front Chamber
18 . 0 By 11 . 0

                              Portico
                              11 . 9 By 5 . 6
area   area

Plan of   Principal Story
50 Feet Front   60 Feet deep.

Scale   10   20   30   40   50   Feet
                                     of

E. Weber & Co. Balto

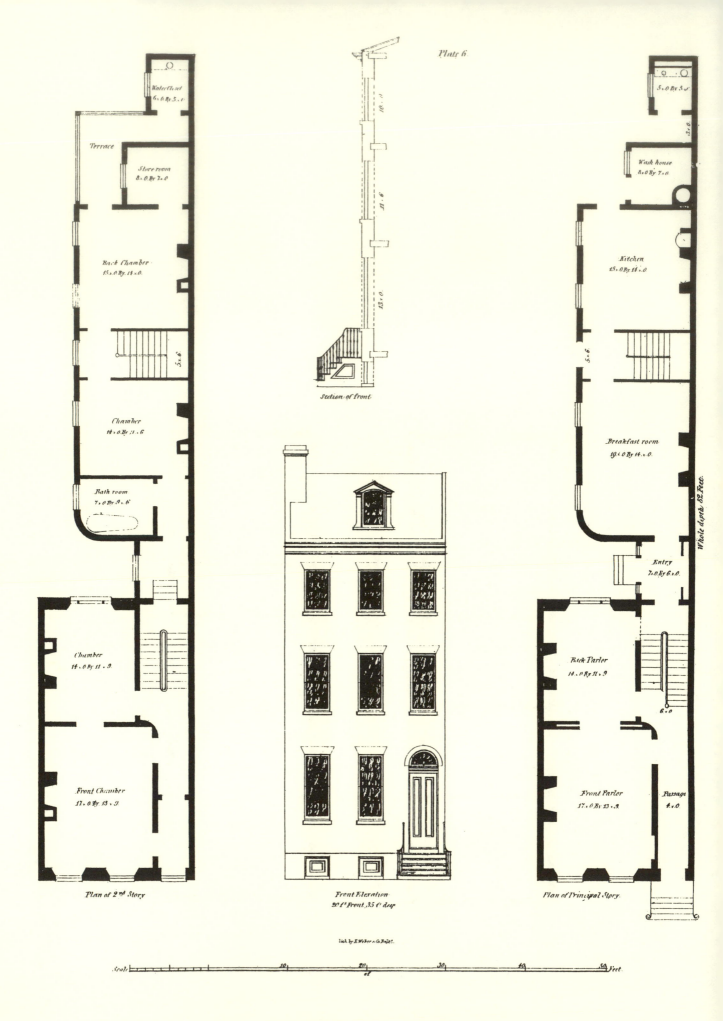

Plate 6

Water Closet
6. 0. By 5. 0.

Terrace

Store room
8. 0. By 7. 0.

Back Chamber
15. 0. By 14. 0.

Chamber
14. 0. By 11. 6.

Bath room
7. 0. By 9. 6.

Chamber
14. 0. By 11. 9.

Front Chamber
17. 0. By 13. 9.

Plan of 2nd Story

Section of front.

Front Elevation.
20 ft Front, 35. 0 deep.

5. 0. By 5. 0.

Wash house
8. 0. By 7. 0.

Kitchen
15. 0. By 14. 0.

Breakfast room
19. 0 By 14. 0.

Entry
7. 0. By 6. 0.

Whole depth 82 Feet.

Back Parlor
14. 0. By 11. 9.

Front Parlor
17. 0. By 13. 9.

Passage
4. 0.

Plan of Principal Story.

Lith. by E. Weber & Co. Balto.

Scale   10   20   30   40   50 Feet.

Plate 2.

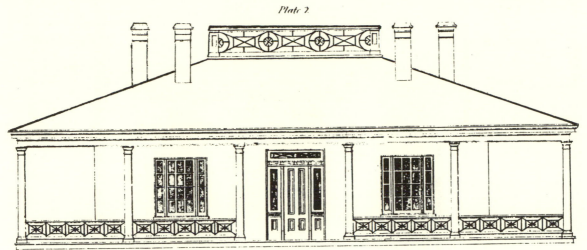

Front Elevation.

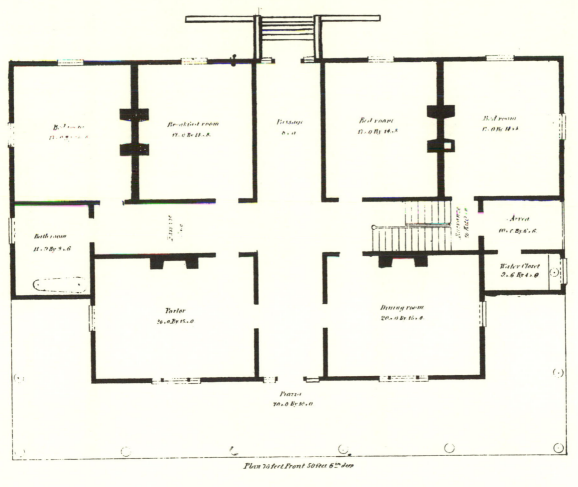

Plan 78 feet Front 50 feet 6¾ deep

Engr by J. Weber & Bull.

Scale ___ *10* ___ *20* ___ *30* ___ *40* ___ *50* | *Feet*

Plate 8.

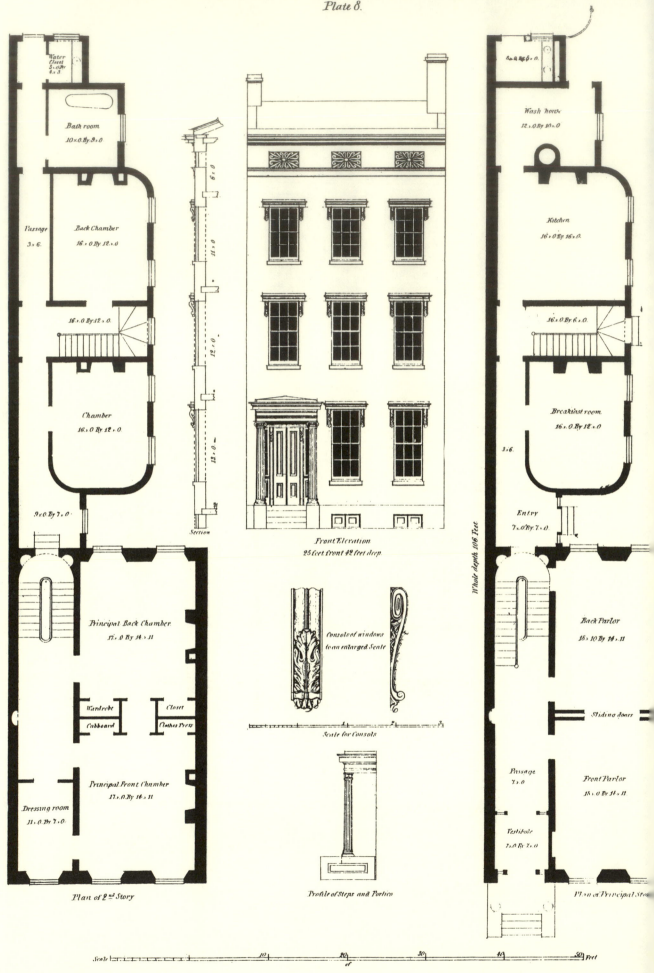

Water
Closet
5 × 0 By
4 × 3

Bath room
10 × 0 By 9 × 0

Passage
3 × 6.

Back Chamber
16 × 0 By 12 × 0

16 × 0 By 12 × 0

Chamber
16 × 0 By 12 × 0

9 × 0 By 7 × 0

6 × 0

11 × 0

12 × 0

13 × 0

Section

Principal Back Chamber.
17 × 0 By 14 × 11

Wardrobe   Closet

Cubboard   Clothes Press

Principal Front Chamber.
17 × 0 By 14 × 11

Dressing room
11 × 0 By 7 × 0

Plan of 2nd Story

Front Elevation
25 feet front 42 feet deep.

Consols of windows
to an enlarged Scale

Scale for Consols

Profile of Steps and Portico

Whole depth 106 Feet

Wash house
12 × 0 By 10 × 0

Kitchen
16 × 0 By 16 × 0

16 × 0 By 6 × 0

Breakfast room.
16 × 0 By 12 × 0

3 × 6.

Entry
7 × 0 By 7 × 0

Back Parlor
18 × 10 By 14 × 11

Sliding doors

Passage
7 × 0

Front Parlor
18 × 0 By 14 × 11

Vestibule
7 × 0 By 7 × 0

Plan of Principal Story

Scale   10   20   30   40   50 Feet

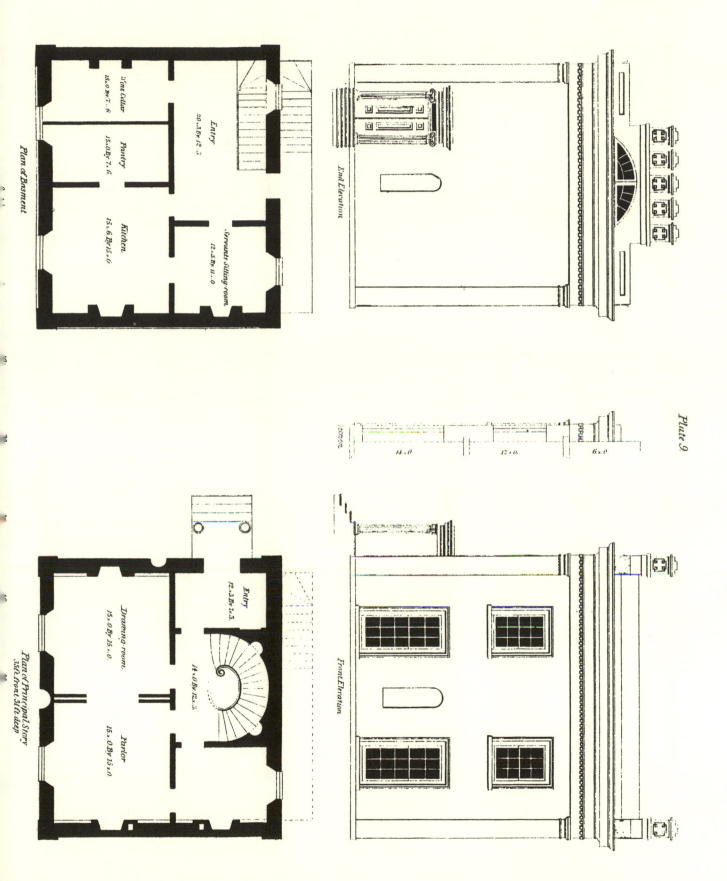

Plan of Basment

Wine Cellar
15.0 By 7..6

Pantry
15.0 By 7..6

Kitchen
15..6 By 15..0

Entry
20..1 By 12..3

Servants Sitting room.
12..3 By 11..0

End Elevation

Plan of Principal Story
35ft front 31ft deep

Drawing room
15..0 By 15..0

Parlor
15..0 By 15..0

Entry
12..3 By 12..3

14..0 By 12..3

Front Elevation

14..0   12..0   6..0

Plate 9

Plate 10.

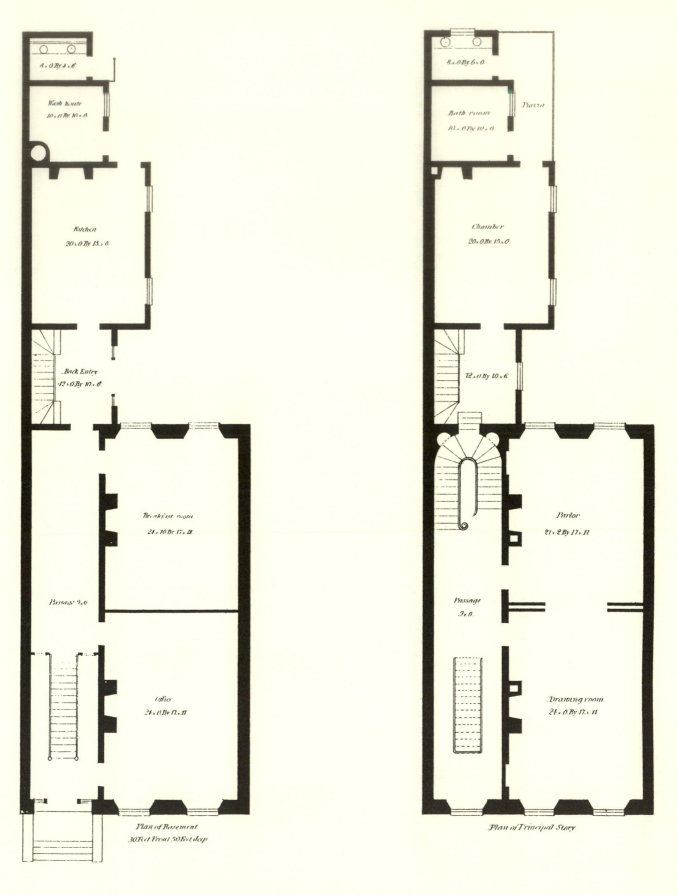

4 . 0 By 4 . 6"

Wash house
10 . 0 By 10 . 0

8 . 0 By 6 . 0

Bath room
10 . 0 By 10 . 0

Piazza

Kitchen
20 . 0 By 13 . 0

Chamber
20 . 0 By 13 . 0

Back Entry
12 . 0 By 10 . 6

12 . 0 By 10 . 6

Breakfast room
24 . 10 By 17 . 11

Parlor
21 . 2 By 17 . 11

Passage 9 . 0

Passage
9 . 0

Office
24 . 0 By 17 . 11

Drawing room
24 . 0 By 17 . 11

Plan of Basement
30 Feet Front 50 Feet deep

Plan of Principal Story

Scale   10   20   30   40   50 Feet

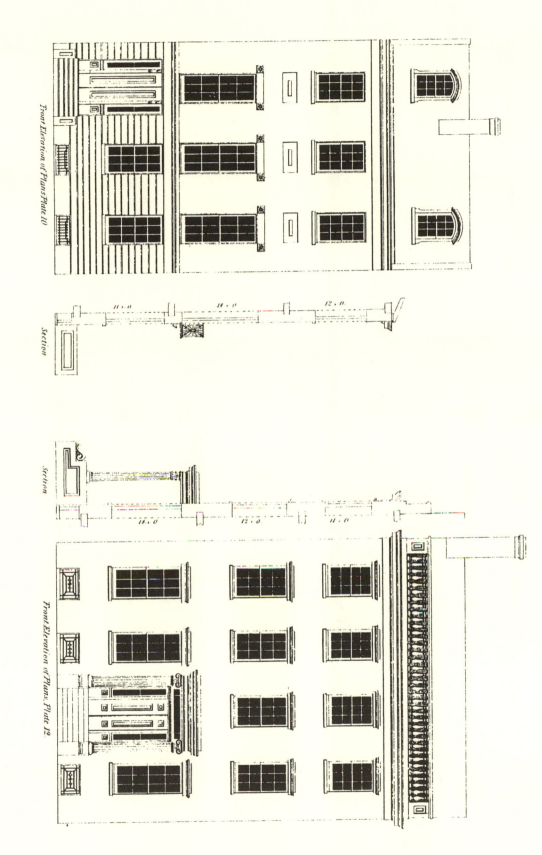

Plate 11.

Front Elevation of Plans;Plate 10.

Section

Section

Front Elevation of Plans;Plate 12.

Scale

Feet

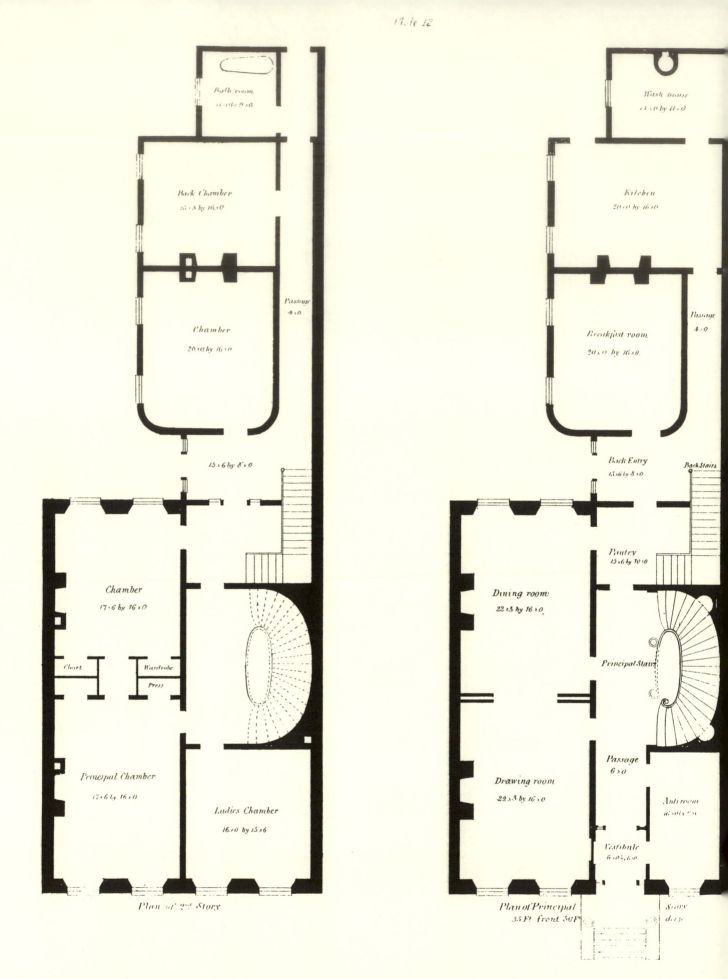

Plate 12

Bath room
11.0 by 9.6

Back Chamber
18.8 by 16.0

Chamber
20.0 by 16.0

Passage
4.0

15.6 by 8.0

Chamber
17.6 by 16.0

Closet   Wardrobe
          Press

Principal Chamber
17.6 by 16.0

Ladies Chamber
16.10 by 15.6

Plan of 2nd Story

Wash house
11.0 by 11.0

Kitchen
20.0 by 16.0

Breakfast room
20.0 by 16.0

Passage
4.0

Back Entry
15.6 by 8.0

Back Stairs

Pantry
15.6 by 10.0

Dining room
22.3 by 16.0

Principal Stairs

Passage
6.0

Drawing room
22.3 by 16.0

Anti room

Vestibule
6.0

Plan of Principal Story
35 Ft front 50 Ft deep

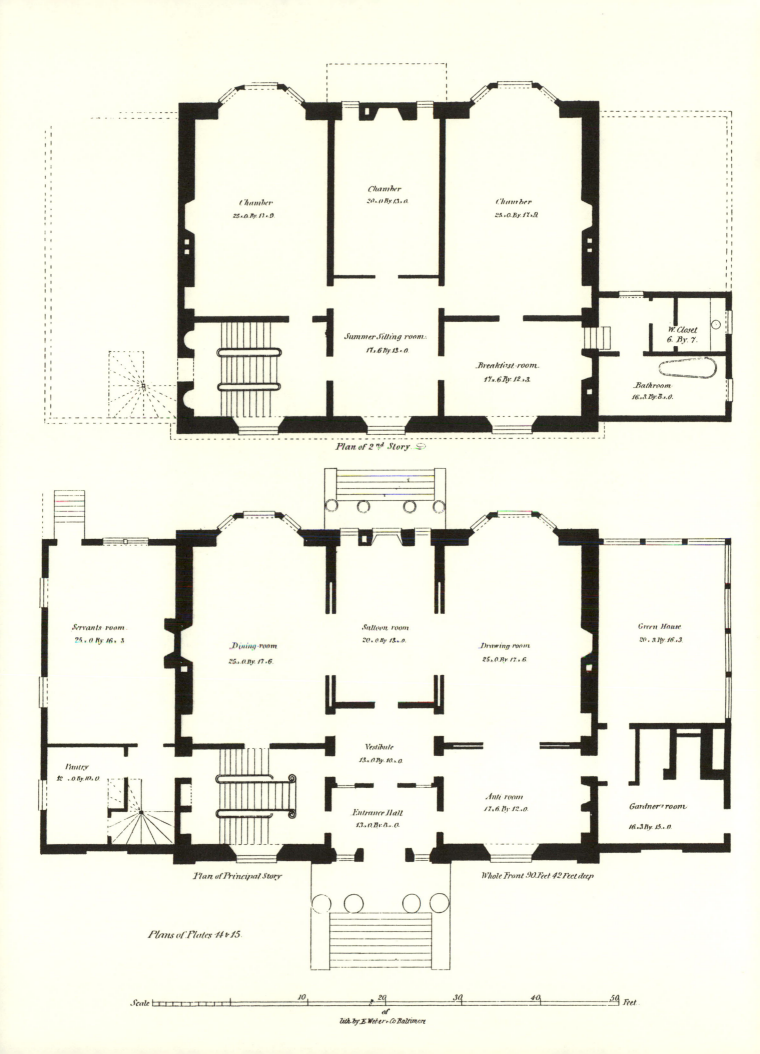

Chamber
25 . 0 By 17 . 9 .

Chamber
20 . 0 By 13 . 0 .

Chamber
25 . 0 By 17 . 9 .

W. Closet
6 . By 7 .

Summer Sitting room
17 . 6 By 13 . 0 .

Breakfast room
17 . 6 By 12 . 3 .

Bathroom
16 . 3 By 8 . 0 .

Plan of 2 nd Story.

Servants room
25 . 0 By 16 . 3

Dining room
25 . 0 By 17 . 6 .

Saloon room
20 . 0 By 13 . 0 .

Drawing room
25 . 0 By 17 . 6 .

Green House
20 . 3 By 16 . 3 .

Pantry
12 . 0 By 10 . 0 .

Vestibule
13 . 0 By 10 . 0 .

Anti room
17 . 6 By 12 . 0 .

Entrance Hall
13 . 0 By 8 . 0 .

Gardner's room
16 . 3 By 13 . 0 .

Plan of Principal Story

Whole Front 90 Feet 42 Feet deep

Plans of Plates 14 & 15.

Scale   10   20   30   40   50 Feet.

of

Lith. By E. Weber & Co Baltimore

Plate 14.

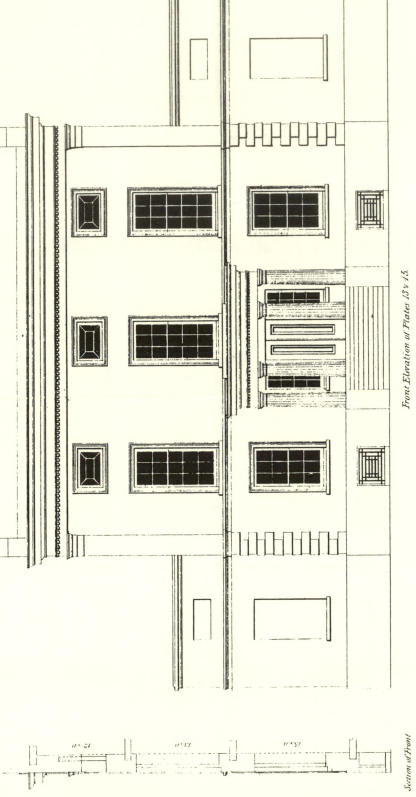

Section of Front

Front Elevation of Plates 13's 15.

Jan Hall

Lith. by E. Weber & Co. Baltimore.

Scale

10   20   30   40   50 Feet

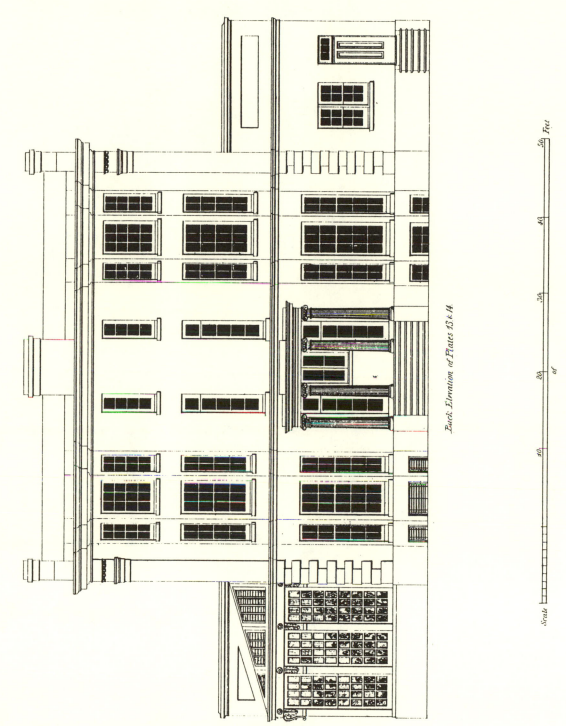

Back Elevation of Plates 13 & 14.

Scale

of

10   20   30   40   50   Feet

Lith. by E.Weber & Co. Baltimore

Plate 16

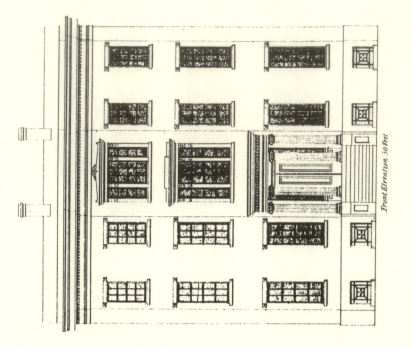

Front Elevation, 30 Feet

Engr. by E. Weber & Co. Balt.

Section

15.0   15.0   11.0   8.0

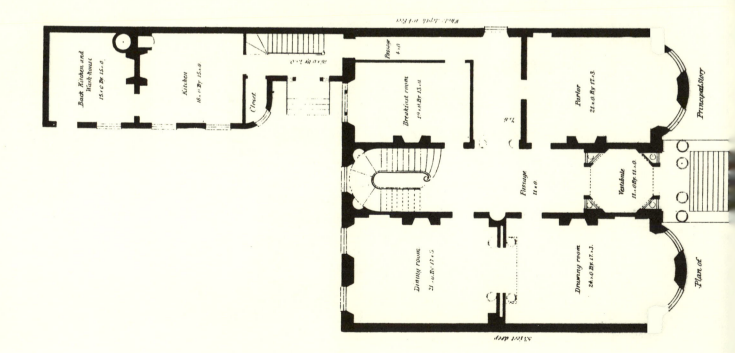

Back Kitchen and Wash house
15.0 By 15.0

Kitchen
18.0 By 15.0

Closet

Breakfast room
19.0 By 15.0

Passage
4.0

Dining room
21.0 By 17.3

Parlor
21.0 By 17.3

Passage
11.0

Vestibule
11.0 By 11.0

Drawing room
24.0 By 17.3

Principal Story

Plan of

Plate 17.

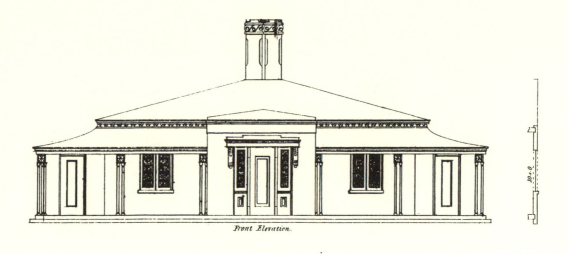

Front Elevation.

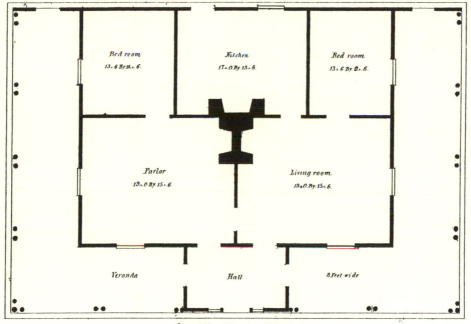

Bed room
13. 6 By 11. 6.

Kitchen
17. 0 By 13. 6.

Bed room
13. 6 By 11. 6.

Parlor
13. 0 By 15. 6.

Living room
13. 0 By 15. 6.

Veranda

Hall

8 Feet wide

Ground Plan 40 Feet Front. 30 Feet deep

Scale [scale bar] 10   20   30   40   50 Feet

Plate 13

Front Elevation

Section

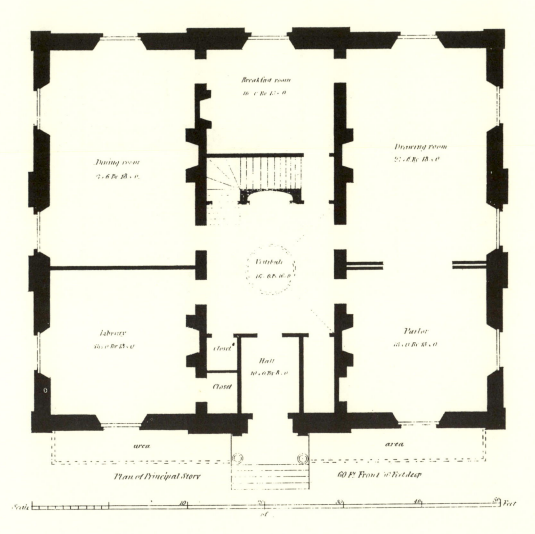

Breakfast room
16.0 By 12.0

Drawing room
21.6 By 18.0

Dining room
21.6 By 18.0

Vestibule
16.0 By 16.0

Library
21.0 By 18.0

closet

Hall
10.0 By 8.0

Closet

Parlor
21.0 By 18.0

area

area

Plan of Principal Story

60 Ft Front 50 Feet deep

Scale   10   20   30   40   50 Feet

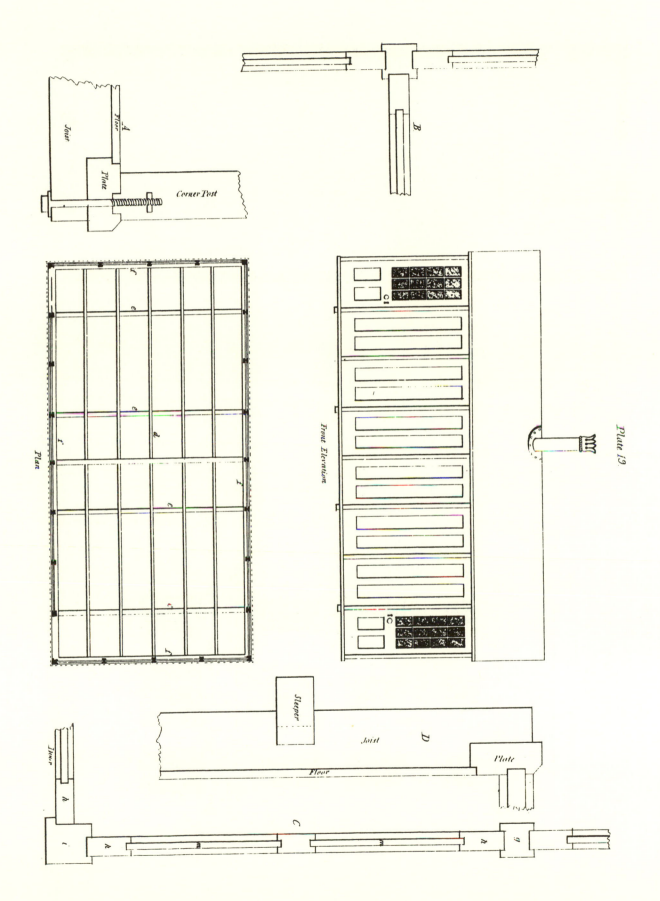

Joist

Floor

A

Plate

Corner Post

B

Plan

r

e

r

e

d

f

c

c

Front Elevation

Plate 19.

Sleeper

Joist

D

Floor

Plate

Floor

h

i

h

C

m

m

h

g

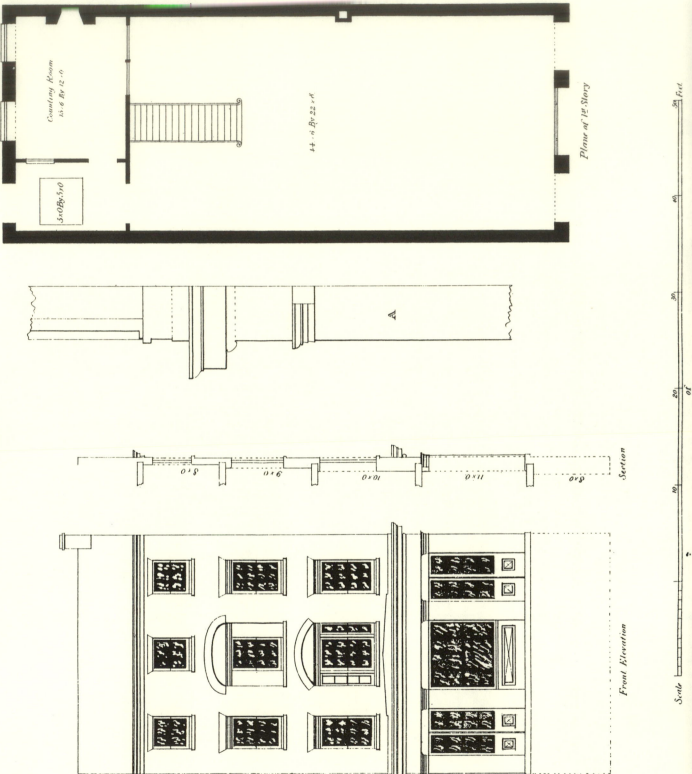

Plate 20

Plane of 1st Story

Counting Room
15·6 By 12·6

5×0 By 5×0

44·6 By 22×4

A

Section

8×0

9×0

10×0

11×0

8×0

Front Elevation

Scale

10   20   30   40   50 Feet

Scale

Plate 21

Front Elevation

Section

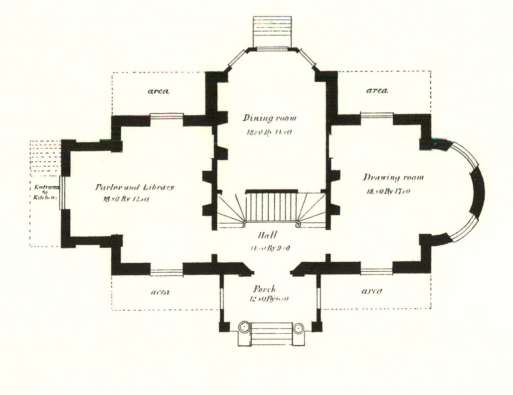

area

area

Dining room
18.0 By 14.0

Parlor and Library
18.0 By 12.0

Drawing room
18.0 By 17.0

Entrance to Kitchen

Hall
14.0 By 9.0

area

Porch
12.0 By 6.0

area

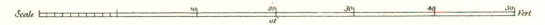

Scale   10   20   30   40   50   Feet

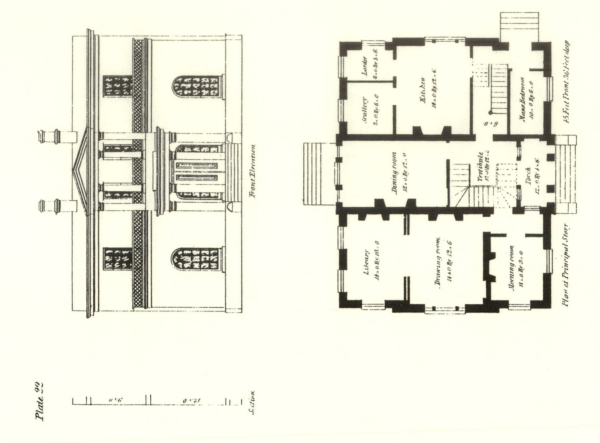

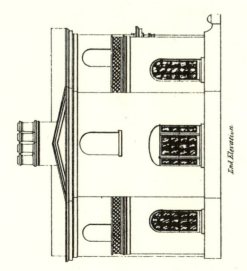

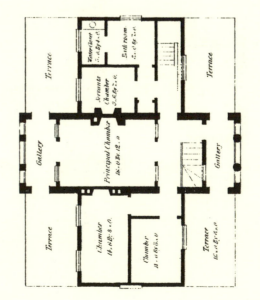

Plate 22

Plate 23

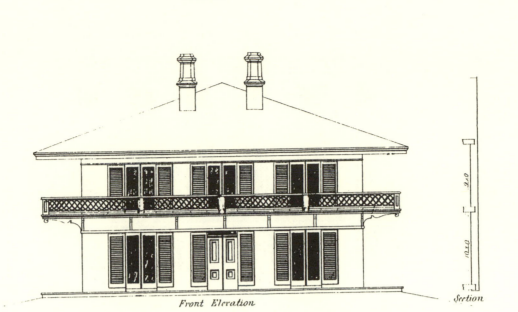

Front Elevation

Section

Kitchen
15.0 by 12.0

Piazza

Parlor
13.6 By 13.6

Sitting room
13.6 by 10.6

Bar

Front Parlor
13.6 by 13.6

Passage
8.0

Bar room
16.0 by 13.6

Piazza

51 wide

Scale   10   20   30   40   50 Feet

Plate 24

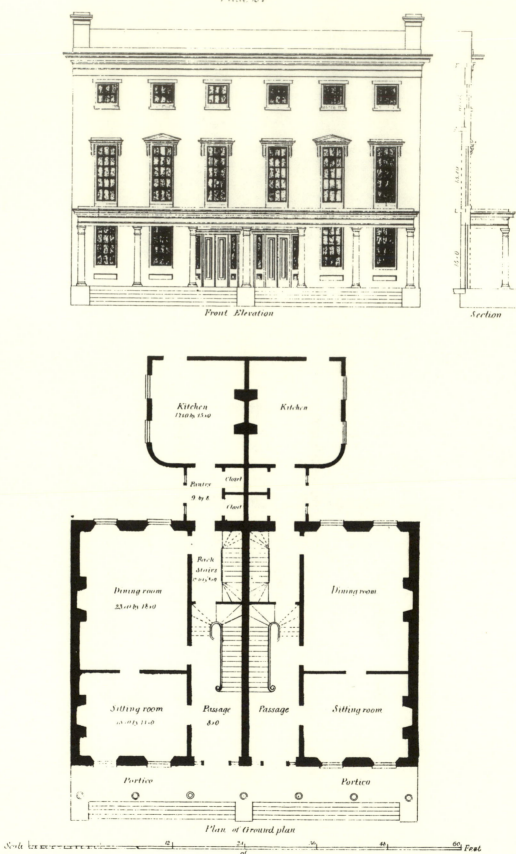

Front Elevation

Section

Kitchen
17.0 by 15.0

Kitchen

Pantry
9 by 8

Closet

Closet

Back
Stairs
6.0 by 5.0

Dining room
23.0 by 18.0

Dining room

Sitting room
18.0 by 14.0

Passage
8.0

Passage

Sitting room

Portico

Portico

Plan of Ground plan

Scale   12   24   36   48   60   Feet
                          of

A

NEW AND CONCISE

METHOD OF HAND-RAILING,

UPON CORRECT PRINCIPLES;

SIMPLIFIED TO THE CAPACITY OF EVERY

PRACTICAL CARPENTER:

ALSO,

A FULL DEVELOPMENT OF THE CYLINDRIC SECTIONS,

AS APPLIED TO

NICHES, GROINS, DOMES,

AND ALL THE

Most Intricate Parts of Carpentry.

By JOHN HALL, ARCHITECT,

AUTHOR OF A SERIES OF DESIGNS FOR DWELLING HOUSES, THE CABINET MAKERS' ASSISTANT, &C.

BALTIMORE:

JOHN MURPHY, PRINTER, 146 MARKET STREET.

::::::::::::::

1840.

PREFACE.

The principles of Hand-Railing, as treated of by many authors, (although in a very able manner) require for their demonstration a degree of mathematical knowledge, which, if not of a very high order, is often beyond the capacity of the Carpenter, who wishes to apply them to practice. The quantity of lines required for the development of a face mould, which so generally embarrass the mind of the student, have been entirely dissipated by the introduction of the Concentric Ellipsograph, invented by the author, and for which he has the satisfaction of being honored with the approbation of a number of scientific persons, as being the most correct and simple method of obtaining the cylindric sections, ever before discovered. One of the important uses of the Concentric Ellipsograph is the facility which the uninstructed artizan perceives in its application to obtain the various curves required in carpentry. There has been shown on most of the plates, one face mould, obtained on the most improved old method, and one on the new; for the latter, the heights taken from the falling moulds and applied to the chords of the plan, to get the pitch of the face moulds, being all that is required; the form of the face mould is procured by the instrument.   The Carpenter will perceive that when he can draw a falling mould for any stairs, the greatest difficulty is overcome.   In furnishing such drawings and explanations as are connected with the following treatise, it has been the object of the Author to be understood by the most inexperienced; in doing this he has made occasional sacrifice of that diction and orderly arrangement which a learned person would prefer.

PLATE I.

TO DRAW THE SCROLL OF A HAND-RAIL.

In Fig. A. let d, c, be the width of the scroll; divide the width into nine equal parts; take one of these parts and place it from c, to a; or d, to b: draw the line a, b, and the diagonal line c, b; come down five parts from d, and draw a line at right angles to d, c; bisect this line, and draw a semi-circle, from the angle x, and through the point where the semi-circle crosses the diagonal line at o, draw a line to meet d, c; draw another line from the angle at 5, through the intersection of the semi-circle and diagonal at o, and produce it to an indefinite length, from the point where the line x, o, touches the line c, d; draw a line at right angles to c. d. to meet the line 5. o. and continue to draw lines at right angles to each other from the points where they intersect the cross lines, until the right number of centres are acquired.   Fig. E. shows the centre's full size for practice and laid in the same position as those of Fig. A. and regularly numbered as the operator progresses to draw the scroll, the centre at 1, draws from b, round to e; the centre 2, draws from e to c; the centre 3, draws from c to f; the centre 4, draws from f to g; the centre 5, draws from g to h; and the centre 6, draws from h to i, which completes the convex side of the scroll.   Set the width of the rail in from b to m, and begin with the same centre 1 as drew the convex side, to draw the concave side, and progress with the same centres until the scroll is completed.   The dotted lines shew the riser, string and projection of the nosing drawn by the same centres as the scroll.

B

TO DRAW THE CURTAIL STEP.

Fig. C.   Take the same centres as for the scroll.   Set the distance the string and riser is in from the scroll and the projection of the nosing, and draw them equidistant from the scroll, which will give the form of the curtail step and riser.

TO DRAW THE FACE MOULD FOR THE SCROLL.

Place the pitch board as in Fig. B, and draw lines at right angles to the bottom of the pitch board, at discretion; then take the length of the line *a*, 7, on the longest side of the pitch board, and lay it down at *a*, 7, in Fig. D; place the different divisions of the line *a*, 7, on Fig. B, on the line *a*, 7, Fig. D, and draw lines at right angles to it, to an indefinite length; then take the different lengths of the lines on each side of the pitch board *o*, 7, Fig. B, and place them respectively on the lines in Fig. D, as the letters and numbers indicate, and through those points transferred from Fig. B, trace round the form of the face mould.

TO FIND THE FALLING MOULD.

Fig. G.   Lay down the pitch board and divide the height into six equal parts; draw the line 1, 6, equal to one of those parts from the bottom of the pitch board.   This allows for the level part of the eye of the scroll.   The distance of the line *b*, from *c*, is from the face of the riser to the beginning of the twist.   Take the length round from *a* to *x*, on Fig. B, and apply it to Fig. G, from *b* to 6″.   Divide the level of the scroll from *o* to 6″ into any number of equal parts, and near about the length of the rake of the pitch board into a like number of parts, and get the curve of the top edge of the mould, by intersecting lines; then draw another line parallel to the top, to the depth of the rail, and the falling mould is completed.   The outside falling mould may be found in the same way by taking the length of the curve part of the concave part of the rail, and applying it in like manner as for the inside mould, but this one mould will be found sufficient for general purposes.

PLATE II.

TO FIND THE MOULDS FOR CONSTRUCTING A RAIL FOR A STAIRS WITH A LEVEL PLATFORM.

Commence by laying down the plan of the rail, Fig. 1, with as much of the straight part of the rail attached to the curve part as may be desired; find the stretch out of the convex side of the rail by dividing the radius of the circle from the centre to 4. into four equal parts. Come down three parts and from it draw a line to touch the extreme of the diameter, and produce it to an indefinite length. Draw a tangent parallel to the diameter line, to meet the indefinite line, and from where they intersect to the point C. will be equal to the length of the quarter circle. Take this length and lay it off on each side of the centre plumb line, Fig. 2, as E. F.; apply a pitch board at each end of the stretch out, one supposed to be on the last step of the first flight, and the other elevated on the first step of the return flight. Join the angles of the pitch boards that are nearest to each other by the line *u. u.* Curve off the angles, either by the common method of intersecting lines, or with the compasses, and the bottom edge of the falling mould will be completed. Draw a line parallel to the bottom, for the top of the mould; place the length of the straight part of the rail outside the stretch-out diameter lines, from F. to V. and E. to *g;* from V. *g.* raise plumb lines to cut the falling mould and square off the ends of the falling mould, inside those plumb lines and the falling mould will be completed.

TO FIND THE FACE MOULD.

At Fig. 2. bisect the centre plumb line from 3. the top of the falling mould to the bottom edge, and through the centre draw the line *o. z.* at right angles to the falling mould; bring down the corners of the falling mould, as shown by the dotted lines, to touch the convex side of the plan of the rail, Fig. 1. Then draw them to the centre, find the centre of the thickness of the plan of the rail, as shown by the dotted line, from each end of the centre of the rail; draw the dotted chord line; and parallel to it, draw another line to touch the lowest corner of the rail, as *x. s.*; draw a line from the centre, at right angles to the two chord lines, to cut the convex side of the rail, and through this intersection draw a line from the point 3″ and produce it to the tangent stretch-out line; from it raise a plumb line to the top of the falling mould. This will be the centre height to apply to the centre height of the face mould. Raise plumb lines from the chord line *s*, on Fig. 1, at *o. o.* and *g. g.*; take the heights from the falling mould, *o. o. b.* 2. and *g. g.* and apply them to the corresponding heights from the chord line, Fig. 1; these will be the pitch heights for the face mould; through the two outside heights draw the line *w. w.* From the centre height at 2″ as a centre, describe a circle to touch the pitch line, *w. w.*; let fall the tangent dotted line, *r.* 5″, to cut the chord line at 5″; draw the line *e″* 5″ through the centre height at 2″, draw a line at right angles to the pitch line *w. w.*, take the length of the line *e″* 5″ and apply it to the right angled line from 5. to *e.*; draw a line from the point where the centre height cuts the pitch line *w. w.* to the length of the right angled line; and it will be the governing ordinate. Take the length of the governing ordinate in the compasses, and with *e″* as a centre, describe a segment to cut the chord line at 5″; draw a line from this intersection to the centre that produced it at *e″* and this line will be the governing ordinate for the plan of the rail. Draw any number of ordinates parallel to the governing one, from the chord line, to cut the convex side of the rail, and where they intersect the convex side of the rail, raise lines parallel to the pitch heights to cut the pitch line *w. w.*, and let them fall to the concave side of the rail. Where they cut the concave side of the rail, draw lines parallel to the chord line to touch the ordinates, as *k. l. m. n. p.* From the points where the plumb lines cut the pitch line *w. w.*, draw ordinates parallel to the governing one, to an indefinite length; take the lengths of the ordinates on the plan from the chord line to the convex side of the rail, as *x′, y′.* 2′, *b′.* 3′, *c′.* 4′, *d′.* 5″, *e″.* 6′, *b′.* 7′, *g′.* 8′. *h′.* 9′, *i′. s′, t′.* and apply them to the corresponding ordinates for the face mould; through these points trace the convex side of the face mould, take the lengths of the ordinates on the plan from the convex side of the rail to the points where the parallel lines to the chord line cut the ordinates, as *d′, r′. l′, e′. m′, b′. n′, g′.* and *p′, h′.* and apply them to the corresponding letters on the face mould; through those points trace the concave side of the face mould, draw a line from 1. to *y.*, to cut off the end of the face mould, and a line from *j.* to *t.* to cut off the other end. The line *&. b.* shows where the straight part joins to the curve part, which completes the face mould. At A. shew the pitch heights for the upper wreath, taken from the corresponding heights at B. of the falling mould.   The chord line *c. d. e.* at A. is drawn different from that of the other chord line, it being drawn parallel to the centre of each end of the rail piece, but the chord line, *c. d. e.* at A. is drawn to touch the lowest corners of the rail piece, and the upper pitch height taken from the line *e. 5.*, at B. of the falling mould, instead of being taken from the line V. in the usual way.   This arrangement is more simple and where the pitch is not great, will be found sufficiently correct.   The lines shown at A. will be sufficient to obtain the face mould by using a concentric ellipsograph, an instrument which will be hereafter described, and the method of applying it.   In this plate the lower face mould will answer for the upper wreath, because the easings and the pitch of the lower and upper parts of the falling mould correspond with each other.

PLATE III.

TO FIND THE FACE AND FALLING MOULD FOR A STAIRS WHICH HAVE THE STEPS THROWN INTO THE CIRCULAR PART OF THE STRING.

Commence by laying down the plan of the rail, with as much of the straight part attached to the circular part as may be desired, set in the centre baluster *o.*, determine on the width of the tread and set in the balusters around the centre of the rail from *o.* equal to half of the tread, draw the riser on each side next to the diameter in the straight part of the rail *x. x.*   Measure up from the risers, *x. x.* the width of the tread and draw the risers, *u. u;* curve off their ends in the circular part of the string, at discretion, observing that the termination of the curves of the risers tend to the centre of the opening; the dotted line outside the rail shows the projection of the nosings.   The stretch-out is obtained by the same method as at Plate II., by dividing the radius into four equal parts, and measuring down from the diameter line to the point 7, equal to seven of these parts. From the point 7. draw lines to touch the extremities of the diameter at T. V. and produce them to cut the tangent at *t. t.*, then the distance from *t. t.* will be equal to the length around the semi-circle.   The stretch-out of the concave side of the rail is found precisely in the same way for the outside falling mould, which is represented in the elevation, Fig. 2., by the dotted lines.

To draw the inside falling mould, determine on any base line, as M, N.   Carry up plumb lines from the stretch-out *t. t.* to an indefinite length, take the straight part of the rail on Fig. 1. from V, to T. and place it outside the diameter stretch-out line from R. to K. and P. to L.; raise plumb lines from K. L. to an indefinite length; place in the height rod, and draw a pitch-board the same distance outside the stretch-out line R at the bottom, that the riser is outside the diameter line in the straight part of the rail fig. 1.   Also, place a pitch-board at the top, the same distance outside the stretch-out line P, that the first riser is outside the diameter at Z, in the straight part of the rail fig. 1, on the return flight.   Draw the hypotenuse of the pitch-boards and produce them to the stretch-out lines P, R. at *w, w;* draw a line from *w* to *w*, ease off the angles, and the bottom edge of the falling mould will be obtained. Draw a line parallel to the bottom edge; for the top, square off the ends inside the plumb lines K, F, and A, L, and the inside falling mould will be completed.   Proceed by the same method to form the outside falling mould, only instead of taking the stretch-out of the convex side of the rail, take the stretch-out of the concave side; the outside falling mould is indicated by the dotted lines.   The pitch heights for the face mould are always taken from the inside falling mould, the principal use of the outside falling mould being to square the rail, this being the only correct method by which it can be done.

TO DRAW THE FACE MOULD Fig. 3.

Let G represent the semi-plan or half of fig. 1, of which S is the centre.   Draw the dotted chord line from the middle of the thickness of each end of the rail, and parallel to it draw another chord line to touch the lowest corner of the rail piece; raise plumb lines from the chord line, as K F, H C, and also from the centre S to an indefinite length; take the distance *a*, round the convex side of the rail from *h* to *b*, and place it in fig. 2, from R to I, and P to O.   Raise plumb lines from I O, to cut the top of the inside falling mould; divide the centre line into two equal parts where it cuts the top and bottom edges of the falling mould, and through the centre draw a line at right angles to the falling mould; where this line cuts the two edges of the falling mould, bring them down parallel to the centre line to touch the convex side of the rail fig. 1.   From thence draw lines to the centre, and where those lines cross the centre line of the rail, they give the points from which the dotted chord line is drawn; this space on each side of the centre line allows for making a butt joint.   Take the heights H C, I E, K F, Fig. 2, and apply them to the pitch heights H C, I E, K F, Fig. 3.   Draw a line through the points C F, and this line will be the pitch of the face mould. From the point E as a centre, describe a circle to touch the pitch line; bring down the tangent dotted line to cut the chord line, from this intersection to the centre height at *b*, on the convex of the rail; draw the line 9 *b*, from the centre height at E; draw a line at right angles to the pitch line; take the length of the line *b* 9 in G, and apply to the right angled line; from the pitch line to *b*, draw a line from the point where the centre height cuts the pitch-line to the point *b*;—this line will be the governing ordinate for the face mould.   Take the length of this line with your compasses, and at the point *b* in G, as a centre, describe a segment to cut the chord line as at 5; from 5 to the point *b*, draw a line—this line will be the governing ordinate for the plan G.   Draw any number of ordinates parallel to the governing one to cut the chord line, and the convex side of the rail.   Carry up those points *a, b, c, d, e, f, g, h, i*, by lines parallel to the pitch heights, to cut the pitch line at 1, 2, 3, 4, 6, 7, 8, and bring them down to cut the concave side of the rail; from those points draw lines parallel to the chord line, to meet the ordinates at *l, m, n, s, p.* Carry up lines from the corners K. *i, x, a*, of the rail piece G; to meet the pitch-line, from *x*, 1, 2, 3, 4, 6, 7, 8, 0, draw lines parallel to the governing ordinate, to an indefinite length; take the lengths of the ordinates in G, from the chord line to the convex side of the rail, and apply them to the corresponding ordinates from the pitch-line; through those points *a, b, c, d, e, f, g, h, i*, trace the convex side of the face mould, then take the lengths of that part of the ordinates in G from the convex side of the rail *c, d, e, f, g*, to the points *l, m, n, s, p*, and apply them from the corresponding letters on the convex side of the face mould, to the points *l, m, n, s, p*, on the concave side; through those points trace the concave side of the mould; make *o, i* and *x, a* equal to *o, i* and *x, a* in G; draw lines from the concave corners to the points *i, a*, and the face mould will be completed.   The line *r, h* shows where the straight part of the rail commences from the circular part.   Fig. 4, shows the face mould for the upper wreath, the pitch heights J, A, Y, B, D, corresponding with the heights taken from the falling mould J, A, Y, B, D; the chord line J, D, is taken from the plan fig. 1.   Fig. 4 shows all the lines that are necessary when the face mould is to be drawn with an ellipsograph.

PLATE IV.

TO DESCRIBE THE MOULDS FOR A HAND-RAIL FOR A STAIRS WITH A LEVEL LANDING, AND ONE RISER CUTTING INTO THE CIRCULAR PART OF THE STRING.

Draw the plan of the rail fig. 1; determine on the width of the steps, and set the ballusters around from each side of the centre one o, in the middle of the rail, equal to half of the tread; draw the riser nearest to the diameter in the straight part of the rail; set up the width of the tread, and draw the riser in the circular part; curve off the end of the riser to suit the balluster.   To draw the inside falling mould, find the length of the convex part of the rail from V around to W, and lay it on any base line from X Y; take the straight part of the rail on the plan from U to V, or T to W, and place it on the base line from Y to F and X to U; draw lines from the points U, X, Y, F, to an indefinite length, perpendicular to the base lines.   Set in the pitch-board on the base line from Y, the same distance the front of the riser is in the straight part of the rail from the diameter line on fig. 1.   Draw the level part of the rail o, o'' to the heighth required, to meet the stretch-out diameter line.   Carry up the line of the hypotenuse of the pitch-board to meet the stretch-out diameter line Y at .P   Join P, O'', ease off the angles, and the bottom edge of the falling mould is obtained.   Draw a line parallel to the bottom for the top edge; square off the lower end inside the line F, L.   Carry up the centre line to cut the top of the falling mould.   Bisect the centre line where it cuts the bottom and top of the falling mould, and draw the joint through the centre at right angles to the falling mould; bring down lines from each corner of the joint to touch the convex side of the plan fig. 1; from thence draw lines to the centre; draw the dotted line *m, n,* and parallel to it draw the chord line to touch the lowest corner of the rail. Draw a line from the centre at right angles to the chord line, to cut the convex side of the rail at P; take the length around from V to P, and apply it on the base line from Y to E and X to R.   Raise plumb lines from E R to cut the top of the falling mould;—these are the centre heights of the falling mould, to be applied to the centre heights of the face moulds.   The dotted lines in the elevation show the outside falling mould—the heights for the outside falling mould being always the same as for the inside falling mould; the only difference in laying the former down is by taking the stretch-out of the concave side of the rail, and placing it on the base line as indicated by the dotted lines *s, s.*

TO FIND THE FACE MOULD.

At fig. 3 let S represent the semi-plan *z, z,* the chord line drawn parallel to the dotted line, to touch the lowest corner of the rail piece, from the centre of each end of the rail piece; raise the lines D, F, to an indefinite length, perpendicular to the chord line *z, z;* also, draw a line from the centre O perpendicular to the chord line.   Take the heights D, I. E, K. F, L. from fig. 2, and apply them to the lines D, E, F, fig. 3; draw a line through the two outside heights at I, L, which will be the pitch-line of the face mould.   Set the compasses in the centre height and describe a circle to touch the pitch-line; bring down the dotted tangent line to S to cut the chord line.   At *o* draw a line from *o* to *e;* draw a line through the centre height at K perpendicular to the pitch-line; take the length of the line *o, e,* at S, and cut off the length of the line *t, e,* on the face mould; draw a line from *e* to the point *o* where the centre height cuts the pitch line—this line will be the governing ordinate.   Take the length of this ordinate with the compasses, and with *e* in *s* as a centre, describe a segment to cut the chord line at *o;* draw a line from *o* to *e* for the governing ordinate; draw any number of ordinates parallel to the governing one, and where they cut the convex side of the rail piece S at *a, b, c, d, e, f, g, h.*   Carry up lines to cut the pitch-line at R, *l, m, n, p, r, i',* and bring them down to cut the concave side of the rail piece S, from the points R, *l, m, n, p, r, i';* raise lines parallel to the governing ordinate; carry up the two corners *i.* 1, and the point 7 of the rail piece S, to meet the pitch-line; from

D

thence draw lines parallel to the other ordinates. Take the lengths of the ordinates in the rail piece S, and apply them to the corresponding ordinates from the pitch-line, and through those points trace the convex side of the face mould; make b 2, c 3, &c. on the face mould equal to b 2, c 3, &c. on S, and through those points draw the concave side of the face mould. Draw a line from i to h, and 1' to a, for the ends of the face mould. This, and the preceding face moulds are drawn with the plank sprung.

Fig. 4 shews the method of getting the pitch of the face mould for the upper wreath, the spring of the plank, &c. when it is to be struck with the ellipsograph. The pitch heights A G, B H, C, correspond with those of the inside falling mould, from which as in all cases they are taken; the spring bevel shown in the semi-plan exhibits plainly how the spring is obtained; although it is obtained different from fig. 3 in plate 5, it will be found sufficiently correct—as it has a tendency to make the spring greater, in consequence of the convexity of the face mould being farther from the chord line than the semi-plan; but in all cases where the easings in the falling mould are not great, the difference can scarcely be perceived.

PLATE V.

TO FIND THE FALLING MOULDS FOR EXECUTING A HAND-RAIL FOR A STAIRS WITH EIGHT WINDERS, THENCE TO FIND THE FACE MOULD.

Fig. 1, the plan of the rail. Find the stretch-out of the convex side of the rail, and place it on any base line at fig. 2; carry up a line from the stretch-out points at S, S, perpendicular to the base line; set in a pitch-board of a straight step, both top and bottom; outside the stretch-out line S, S, draw a line from one pitch-board to the other, ease off the angles, and draw a line parallel to the bottom for the top of the falling mould; square off the ends inside the plumb lines at A and F; carry up the centre line to cut the top and bottom of the falling mould; bisect the centre line at 1, 2 in o, and through o draw a line at right angles to the falling mould. Bring down lines from the points D, 4 to touch the convex side of the rail fig. 1, and then draw them to the centre; the distance those lines are from the centre line allow for making the joint. Draw the dotted chord lines on the plan, and parallel to them draw lines to touch the lowest corners of each rail piece—those lines will be the bases from which the face moulds are to be elevated. Draw lines from the centre of fig. 1 at right angles to the chord lines to cut the convex of the rail at 5, 5, place the distance from the diameter around to 5, on the base line from S to H, and raise plumb lines from the points H, H, to cut the top of the falling mould at B and E—then the points A, B. C, D. E, F. will be the heights for the pitch heights of the face mould.

TO DESCRIBE THE FACE MOULD FOR THE UPPER WREATH.

At Fig. 4 let K represent half of the plan of the rail; raise lines perpendicular to the chord line from the points s, s, t; let D, D be the lower height, B, B the middle height, and A, A the upper height of the face mould, carried over from the falling mould, as shown by the dotted lines. Draw a line in fig. 4 from A to D; take the centre height at B as a centre for the compasses, and describe a circle to touch the pitch-line A, D; bring down the tangent dotted line o, o, to cut the chord line of K at o; draw a line from o to c; draw a line through the centre height B at right angles, to the pitch line A, D; take the length of the line o, c in K, and place it on the line o, c from the pitch-line A, D. Draw a line from c to 3, where the centre height cuts the pitch-line, and it will be the regulating ordinate. Take the length of the regulating ordinate with your compasses, and with c, in K, as a centre, describe a segment to cut the chord line at 3; draw a line from 3 to c, and it will be the regulating ordinate for the semi-plan K; draw the ordinates i, k, 1, a. 2, x. 7, g. and 8, h. parallel to the regulating ordinate, and draw any number of intermediate ordinates; carry up lines perpendicular to the chord line from the points 1, k, x, a, b, c, d, e, f, g, h, to cut the pitch-line at 1, 1', 2', 2, 4, 5, 6, 8, and bring them down to cut the concave side of the rail at u, u, u; draw a line parallel to the chord from the point u, u, u, to cut the ordinates at p, q, r, from the points i, 1', 2', 2, 4, 5, 7, 8, on the pitch-line. Raise lines to an indefinite length parallel to the regulating ordinate 3, c; take the length from i to k in K, and place it from i to k on the pitch-line, also take 1, a. 2 b, 4 d, 5 e, 6 b, 7 g, and 8 h, in K, and from the pitch-line cut off the lengths of the corresponding ordinates; through those lengths draw the convex side of the face mould; take the length of the ordinate 2 x, in K, and apply it to 2 x from the pitch-line; take the lengths of the ordinates from the convex side of the rail in K, as $b\,p$, $c\,u$, $d\,q$, $e\,r$, and apply them from the convex side of the face mould at $b\,p$, $c\,u$, $d\,q$, $e\,r$, then through the points 1, x, p, u, q, r, g; trace the concave side of the face mould, draw a line from g to h, and from 1 to k, and the face mould will be completed—the line $a\,x$ shows where the curved part of the face mould joins the straight part.

Fig. 3 shows the pitch-heights for the upper wreath resting on the same base line as fig. 4; fig. 3 also shows the governing ordinate, the pitch, and spring bevels.   To find the spring bevel, draw any line as the dotted line $a\,b$ at right angles to the pitch line, to cut the dotted line $c\,d$; the line $c\,d$ is drawn parallel to the pitch-line to touch the back of the face mould, as shown in fig. 5; take the radius of the circle drawn from the centre height at B, and with a as a centre, describe a segment to cut the pitch-line, then draw a line from the intersection to the point b, and it will be the spring of the plank.   The governing ordinate is obtained in the same way as already described for fig. 4. The lines in fig. 3 show all that is necessary when the face mould is to be struck with an ellipsogra h.

Fig. 5 exhibits the face mould for the lower wreath, with all the principal lines, bevels, &c. on it, duly explained. The pitch-heights G C, H E, I F, are taken from the corresponding heights on the falling mould.

PLATE VI.

TO DRAW THE FALLING MOULD FOR AN ELLIPTIC STAIRS, THENCE TO FIND THE FACE MOULDS.

The plan Fig. 1, shows the ends of the steps diverging from the rail, which are equally divided around it and the wall.   To find the inside falling mould, take the steps around on the convex side of the rail, from c to b, the conjugate diameter, and stretch them out on the base line at fig. 5, from c to b; set up the height rod with the number of risers there are on the plan fig. 1; draw the top of the last riser in to meet the stretch-out line *b* at *s*.   Set up one riser on the lower stretch-out line *c* at *s*, join *s s*, by a line and produce it to the base line at *y*.   Take the distance from *c* around to *a* on fig. 1, and place it on the base line from *c* to *a*, and ease off the angle as shown; by intersections of lines, produce the line *s s*, to an indefinite length at the top; set up the height of the rail on the level landing, the height required to meet the return flight, or if the rail is to terminate on the level landing, as is intended in this case, make it rather higher; draw the level part of the rail out to meet the line *s, s;* ease off the angle, and draw a line parallel to the bottom, which completes the inside falling mould.   The outside falling mould is obtained from the same heights—the only difference is by taking the stretch-out of the concave side of the plan of the rail for the base line, as shown in the preceding plates.   Determine on the joints in fig. 1 for the number of pieces the rail is to be formed of—(in this case they are three); then draw a chord line from the centre of each joint, and parallel to them draw another line to touch the lower corners of the rail pieces; take the stretch-out on fig. 1 around from the centre line *o* to the joints, and lay them out from the centre *o* on the base line fig. 5.   Raise lines from those points perpendicular to the base line to cut the top of the falling mould.   Bisect those lines where they cut the top and bottom of the falling mould, and through the centre draw lines at right angles to the falling mould; bring down lines from the corners of the joints in the falling mould to the base line, and those lines will be the heights to apply from the chords for the pitches of the face moulds.

To draw the face mould fig. 2, raise lines perpendicular to the chord line in fig. 1, from the centre of each end of the rail piece; take the heights A C, B D, in fig. 5 of the falling mould, and apply them to the heights A C, B D, for the face mould; draw a line through the heights at C, D, which will be pitch-line; raise any number of lines perpendicular to the chord line to cut the pitch-line, and at the points where they cut the pitch-line, raise lines perpendicular to the pitch-line; take the lengths of the ordinates from the chord line to the concave and convex sides of the plan, as 1, 2, 3, and apply them to the corresponding ordinates 1, 2, 3, for the face mould; through those points trace the face mould.   It will be observed that this face mould is drawn different from the preceding ones—the plank not being sprung, which is not necessary in this case, the part of the falling mould that fig. 2 is taken from being quite straight.   The more easing or curvature there is in a falling mould the greater is the advantage derived from springing the plank, as it is not only a

E

saving of material by taking a plank of less thickness, but considerably diminishes labor in the execution of it. Figures 3 and 4 show the face moulds for the other sections of the plan with the plank sprung; the letters of the pitch-heights correspond with those of the falling mould, from which they are taken. The method of drawing those face moulds is precisely the same as the face moulds in the preceding plates, which has been repeatedly explained.

Fig. 6 shows the method of developing a small bracket from a great one, or, a greater from a lesser one. In this case let A be the given bracket for the step, and B the bracket for the winder; draw any number of ordinates at right angles to the top of A; determine on the length of B, and place it on any line drawn from the corner 2; draw a line *o p*, and parallel to it draw all the other ordinates from the ends of the ordinates touching the line 2 *p*; draw lines at right angles to the line 2 *p*; take the lengths of the ordinates on A, and apply to the corresponding ordinates on B, as 12, 43, &c. and through those points draw the form of the bracket B.

PLATE VII.

Figures 8, 9 and 10, show different sections of a concentric ellipsograph. To convey an idea of this instrument, let the reader suppose a pair of compasses opened to any radius: for example, to strike the semicircle at fig. 1; then with that radius, lay one leg of the compasses on the centre line or axis of the cylinder, and moving them lengthwise, at the same time causing them to revolve on the bottom leg—the operation of the instrument will be immediately perceived. Fig. 10 is an end view, *x* the shaft which slides through the grooved piece *o*, and in which the stump is fixed for the centre of the arm 1 to revolve on; 2 shows the arm

1 in another position; 3 shows the upper part of 1 that contains the pencil slided out to strike a larger circle; *a*, screw to adjust the upper part to any radius; *b*, screw to keep the pencil firm.   Fig. 8, top view with the arm that contains the pencil placed in a vertical position, at *p* shows the shaft *x* sliding out of *o, o*.   Fig. 9, side view with the arm standing in a vertical position; 5 shows the pencil farther from the centre to strike a larger circle or the convex side of a face mould; 6 shows the arm 7 moved farther back.   Fig. 7 shows the method of constructing an ellipsograph in the most simple manner and which will answer for every purpose to which it is applicable.   Let *a a* represent a piece of wood one inch square and any length, say three feet; *c, c, c, c*, blocks screwed, or nailed down on the bench or drawing board, between which the strip *a, a*, is to easily slide; S a stump fixed in *a, a; v*, a piece of wood one inch square, which revolves on the screw fixed in the stump S; *i*, shows a pencil placed in *v*, equal from the screw to half the shortest diameter of the curve it is to strike; *h* shows the pencil placed in another hole, the thickness of a rail farther from the screw, to strike the convex side of a face mould.   The application of fig. 7, is shown in the next plate.

Fig. A, shows six different sections of a semi-cylinder standing on the same base, struck with an ellipsograph.   Fig. 1, a section cut at right angles to the axis of the semi-cylinder, and consequently a semi-circle. Fig. 2, a section cut in the direction *a, b*, and at right angles to the plane passing through its axis, produces a semi-ellipsis—*a b* being its conjugate diameter, and *o, o* its transverse radius; fig. 3 a semi-ellipsis also, but its conjugate diameter greater than that of fig. 2.   Fig. 4, a section of a semi-cylinder cut in the direction *e, f*, on a plane passing through its axis, and making an acute angle with that plane.   This section and the succeeding one shows the method of springing the plank for hand-rails.   To present a simple and correct view of those sections, the reader will suppose the whole of the figures to be cut around their curves, and turned up on the lines of their different sections in an erect position.   For example, take fig. 1, and cut through the paper around the circle, and turn it up at right angles on the diameter line; also, figs. 2 and 3 in the same manner at right angles.   Fig. 4 must be turned up and the top of the curve at *x* come plumb over the dotted line *s, s*.   This section makes an acute angle with the axis plane.   Fig. 5 must be turned up until the top of the curve at *m* is plumb over the dotted line *u, u*; this section makes an obtuse angle with the axis plane. Fig. 6 is a section cut in the direction $i\, i$, and making an acute angle with the axis plane, the top of this figure must be turned towards the base until its height corresponds with the radius of the base. When those sections are placed in the positions as described above, the reader will plainly see, that every part of their curves are on a line with each other, and of equal radii from the centre line. The importance of this simple instrument, the concentric ellipsograph, and the facility of its application to the obtaining of the section of a cylinder in any direction whatever, is plainly depicted in the various sections on fig. A. The advantages this instrument has over that of the ordinary trammel, are, that it only requires to be set once—viz: *to the radius of the shortest diameter of the curves it is to strike*, to obtain the various curves in a niche, groined ceiling, dome, face mould for a hand-rail, &c. the angle which the objects make with the axis of the instrument whilst being struck produces their conjugate diameters.

PLATE VIII.

TO OBTAIN THE FACE MOULD FOR A HAND-RAIL WITH AN ELLIPSOGRAPH.

In fig. 3 let c, e. 5, 3. be the pitch-heights of A, plate 2 and d 4 the centre height; fix the instrument on the line of the centre height as $g\, g$; place a block on each outside height 3, 5, and against those blocks fix the board $a\, a$, the bottom edge of which must be the same distance from the centre of the instrument that the chord line is from the centre on the plan as $d\, k$; place the pencil in the arm i, the same distance from the centre that the inside of the rail is from the centre on the plan as $o\, k$; take the arm i in your hand and make it revolve, at the same time keeping the point of the pencil in contact with the surface of the board a, a, and mark the concave side of the mould, move the pencil the width of the rail farther from the centre, and draw the convex side of the mould.   The dotted lines at F show the board turned down in a horizontal position with the lines on it as struck with the instrument.   Take the length of the pitch-line from 5 to 3 on the edge of the board, draw a line from the point 5 to touch the curve line xx, and parallel to it draw another to touch the line at x—this will be the tangent part of the rail.   Carry up lines from the corners of the plan s, s, to cut the pitch-line, and from their intersection raise lines at right angles to the pitch-line, and where they cut the convex side of the rail at w, w, draw lines to the inside corners of the mould, which will give the cut of the ends of the face mould; m shows the arm moved round towards the straight part of the face mould.   It will be observed, that in this case the plank is not sprung, as the board for the face mould is fixed quite plumb for it to be struck with the instrument.

Fig. 2 shows the elevation of fig. 3, with the board placed on the blocks in its right position, on which the face mould is to be struck.

Fig. 1 shows the pitch heights of the upper wreath of plate 3; x,x the board for the face mould; o the square showing that the plank is not sprung; c the pencil, always placed in the arm from the centre d, equal to the inside and outside of the rail on the plan.   Where the easings in the falling mould are not great, it is of no importance to spring the plank, as in the two last cases.   What has been said of the method of finding the face moulds in the two last figures will apply to every variety of face moulds when the plank is not sprung.

TO DRAW A FACE MOULD WHEN THE PLANK IS SPRUNG.

Figure 4.   Let A G, B H, C, represent the pitch-heights of fig. 4, plate 8; x,x the bottom edge of the board for the face mould; take the spring bevel shown at B, and place it against the back of the board x, x, so that the top of the board, when equal to the width from the pitch-line to p, will be plumb over the dotted line o, o; then draw the face mould with the instrument as already described for fig. 3; the distance of the line $o\,o$, from s, is equal from s to H. It is necessary for the top edge of the board to stand out of plumb equal to the spring bevel from the centre pitch-height for it to be struck, so that the ends of the twist will be thrown down or up, as the case may be, to suit the curvature of the falling mould.

F

TO DRAW A FACE MOULD WHEN THE PLANK IS SPRUNG.

Fig. 5.   Let the line *a a*, be the bevel or pitch-line of fig. 5, plate 5, and let the board for the face mould be set over this line, the bottom edge of which must always be the same distance from the centre of the instrument, that the chord line is from the centre on the plan, and let the board rest against the bevel C when it is turned up, with its stock resting on the bench; place the pencil in the instrument the distance from the centre equal to the radius of the concave side on the plan, and draw the concave side of the mould; move the pencil the width of the rail from the centre, and draw the convex side; draw the tangent part of the rail as directed, for fig. 3.   To cut the joints of a face mould when the plank is sprung, let the two concave corners of the mould when cut out, rest on the points *i i*, and the back side of the mould rest against the bevel when it is turned up with its stock on the bench; then cut away the ends of the mould until its convex and concave corners are plumb over the corners of the rail on the plan; the dotted lines *v, v, v,* &c. show lines carried up from the corners of the rail on the plan, as shown from fig. 6.

THE METHOD OF FINDING THE THICKNESS OF STUFF FOR THE TWIST OF FIG. 5, PLATE V.

Figure 6.   Let A represent the semi-plan of the rail.   Carry up plumb lines from the chord line 1, 2, 3, 4, 5, 6, three sections of the semi-plan, 1, 2, and 5, 6, being the ends of the rail, and 3, 4, the middle section on the diameter line, where the easing always occurs; take the heights from the falling mould F, *f. o s*, and C 4, on fig. 2, plate 5, and apply them to the corresponding heights on fig. 6, plate 8, and from those heights draw the three sections of the rail *a, b, c,*—the space those sections occupy between two parallel lines is the thickness of stuff required for the wreath when the plank is not sprung, which is six inches, the rail being three inches wide by two and three-fourths thick. The thickness of the stuff required when the plank is sprung, as in this case, will be equal to the length of the dotted line shown on the section *b*, which is four inches.   By this method the thickness of stuff required for any twist can be obtained.

APPLICATION OF THE MOULDS TO CUT OUT THE TWIST.

Commence by making the edge of the plank straight and square, if the plank is not sprung, but if sprung, the edge must be beveled to suit the spring bevel; then lay the face mould with its corners on the concave side, on a line with the edge of the plank, and mark the form of the face mould on the plank; from the corners of the face mould, draw lines across the edge of the plank with the pitch bevel, and from those lines lay down the face mould on the other side of the plank, and draw its form; cut the plank through to those lines, and dress accurately to them the piece for the twist. Then take the inside falling mould, and bend around on the convex side of the rail piece, observing that the rail will square itself on each end from the concave edge of the falling mould, and from one side of the plank, let the extreme ends of the falling mould be even with the plumb cuts of the rail piece; then mark its form on the rail piece; draw square lines from the extreme ends of the falling mould across the plumb cuts, and apply the concave falling mould to those lines; then mark its form on the rail piece; cut away the superfluous wood on the sides to the lines of the two falling moulds, and the twist is squared. Cut off the ends of the twist to the convex falling mould and the shortest edges of the ends of the twist,—then the twist will be prepared to be moulded into the form required.

TO DRAW THE STRING.

The mode of proceeding to obtain the easings on the lower edge of the string, is precisely the same as for the falling moulds, viz. by drawing the face of the string on the plan of the rail and stretching it out on a base line, then apply the same heights as for the falling moulds.

FINIS.

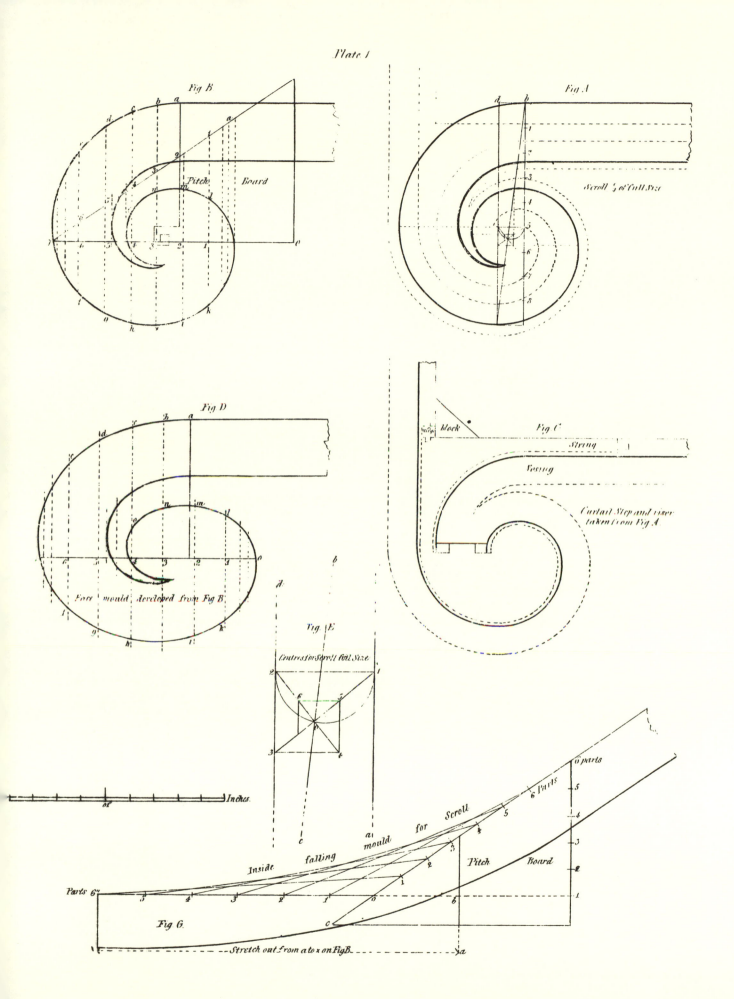

Plate 1

Fig B

Pitch Board

Fig A

Scroll ⅓ of full Size

Fig D

Face mould developed from Fig B

Fig C

block

String

Nosing

Curtail Step and riser taken from Fig A.

Fig E

Centres for Scroll full Size

Inches.

6 parts

6 Parts

Scroll

for

mould

falling

Inside

Parts 6"

Pitch Board

Fig G.

Stretch out from a to x on Fig B

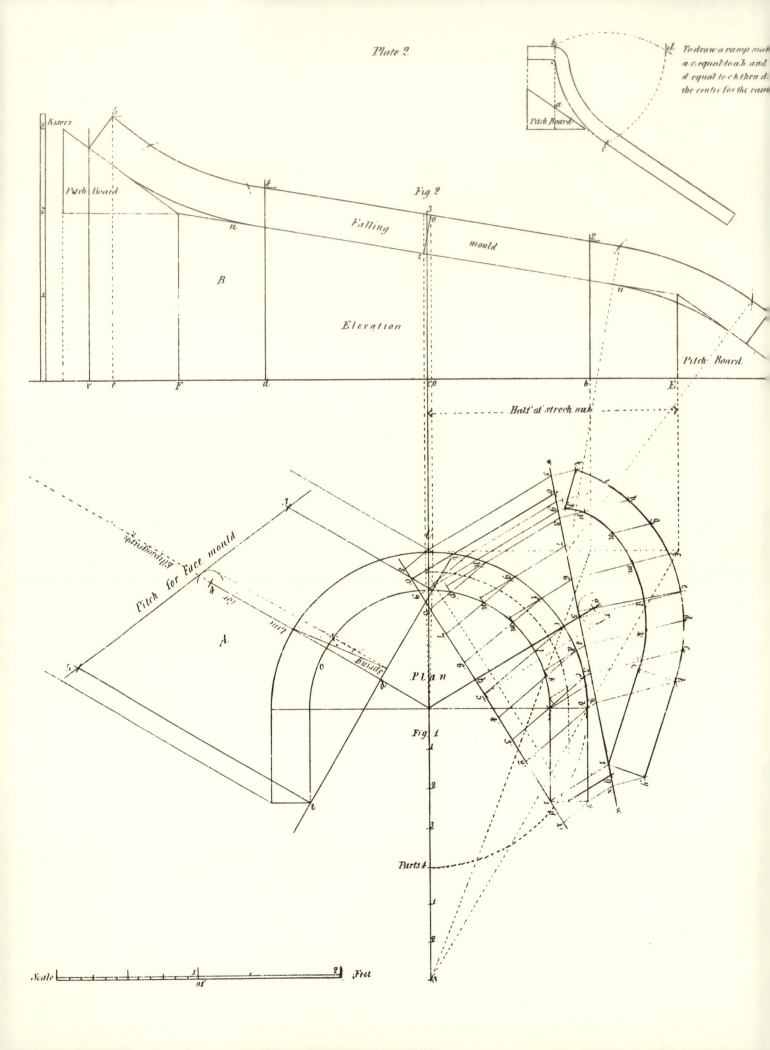

Plate 2

To draw a ramp ...
a c. equal to a h. and ...
d. equal to c h. then d. ...
the centre for the ram...

Pitch Board

Risers

Pitch Board

Fig 2

Falling

mould

B

Elevation

Pitch Board.

Half of strech out

Pitch for Face mould

Handraileing

A

Spring

Plan

Fig 1

Parts 4

Scale   Feet

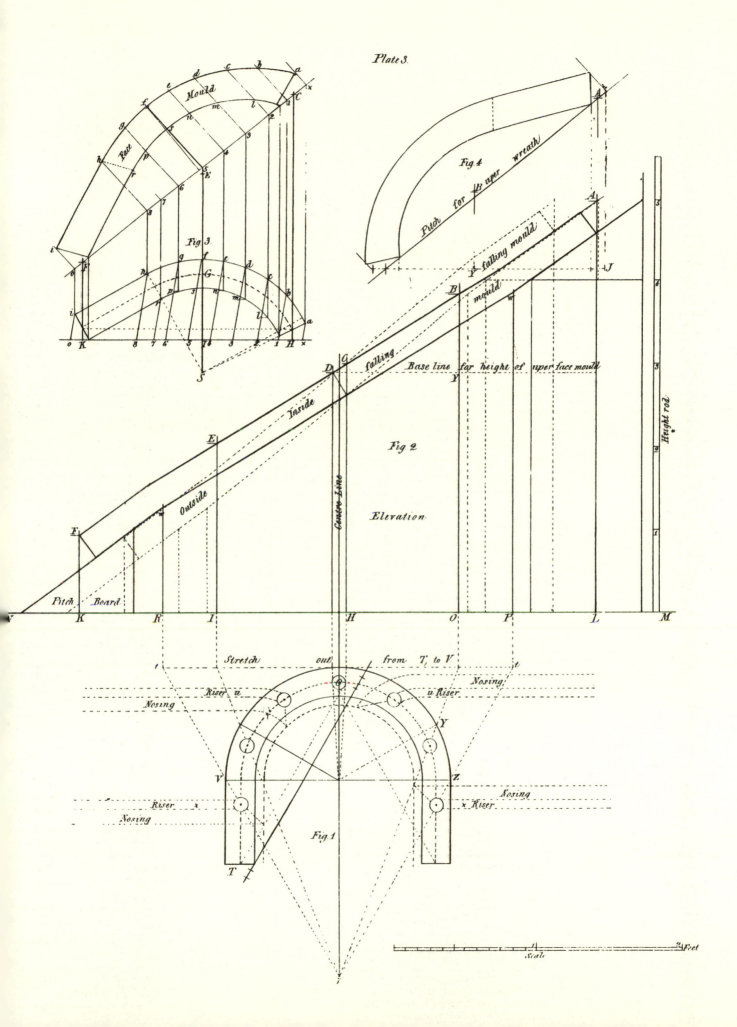

Plate 3.

Mould

Fig 3.

Fig. 4

Pitch for B upper wreath

falling mould

mould

Inside falling

Base line for height of upper face mould

Fig 2

Centre Line

Elevation

Outside

Pitch Board

Height rod.

v   K   R   I   H   O   P   L   M

Stretch   out   from T. to V.

Nosing

Riser u   u Riser

Nosing   Nosing

Y

V   Z

Riser x   x Riser Nosing

Nosing

Fig. 1

T

Scale   Feet

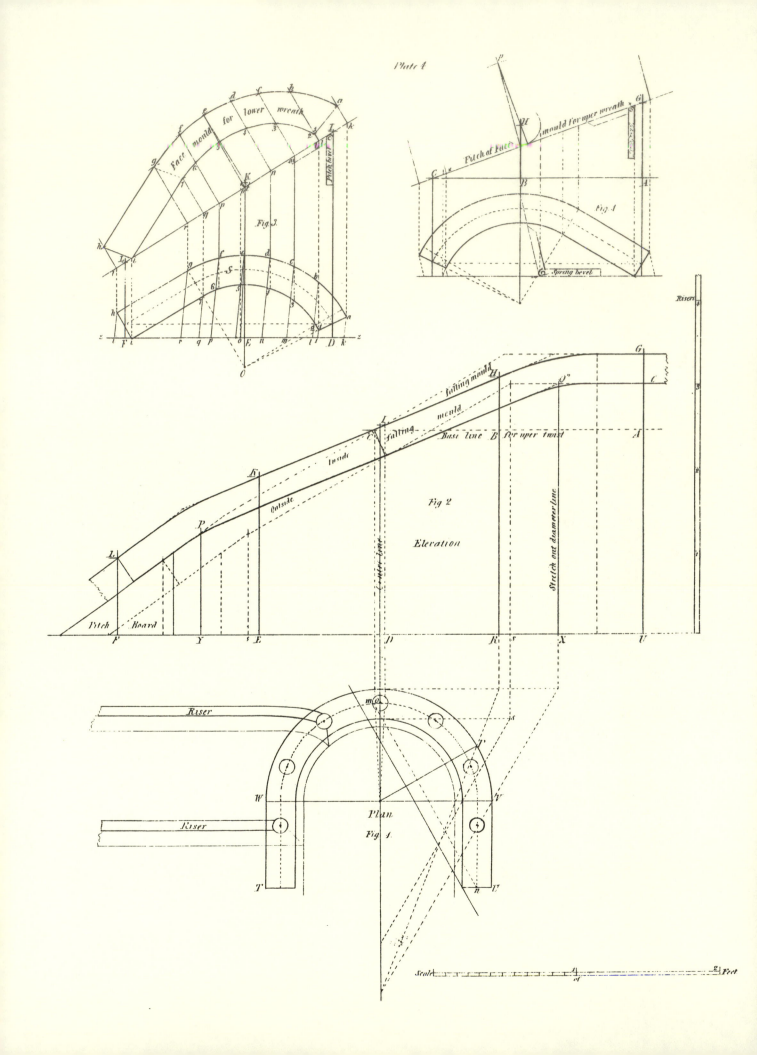

Plate 4

Face mould for lower wreath

Fig. 3.

Pitch bevel

mould for uper wreath

Pitch of Face

Spring bevel

Fig. 4

Risers

Falling mould

falling mould

G

C

Inside

Base line B For uper twist

A

Outside

Center line

Stretch out diameter line

Fig 2

Elevation

Pitch Board

F Y s E D R s X U

Riser

m

Plan.

Fig. 1.

W v

Riser

T V

Scale 4 Feet

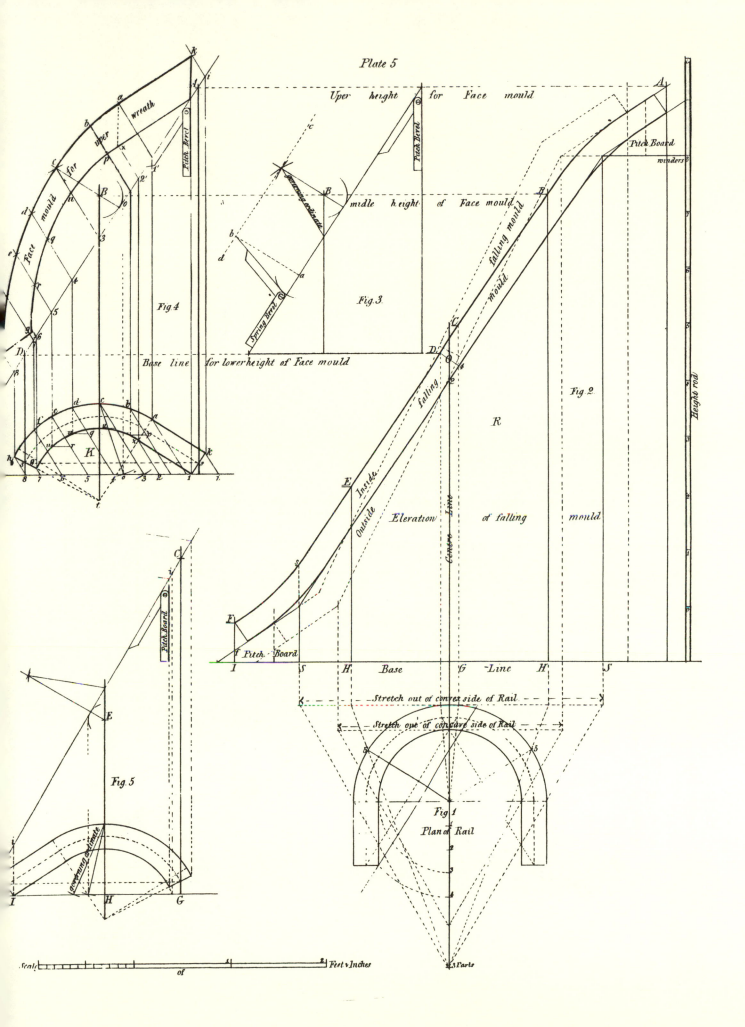

Plate 5

Uper   height   for   Face   mould

Pitch Berel

middle   height   of   Face   mould

spring Berel   B

b

d   a

Fig.3.

Uper   wreath

Face   mould   for

Fig.4.

Pitch Berel

Base   line   for lower height of Face mould

K

falling   mould

Pitch Board

winders

Pitch Board

A

B

C

D

falling mould

Inside

Outside

Elevation   Centre Line   of falling   mould

Fig.2.

R

E

Height rod

Fig.5

Pitch Board

C

E

governing ordinate

I   H   G

Pitch Board

F   f Pitch Board

I   S   H   Base   G   Line   H   S

Stretch out of convex side of Rail

Stretch out of concave side of Rail

Fig 1
Plan of Rail

Scale   of   Feet & Inches   Parts

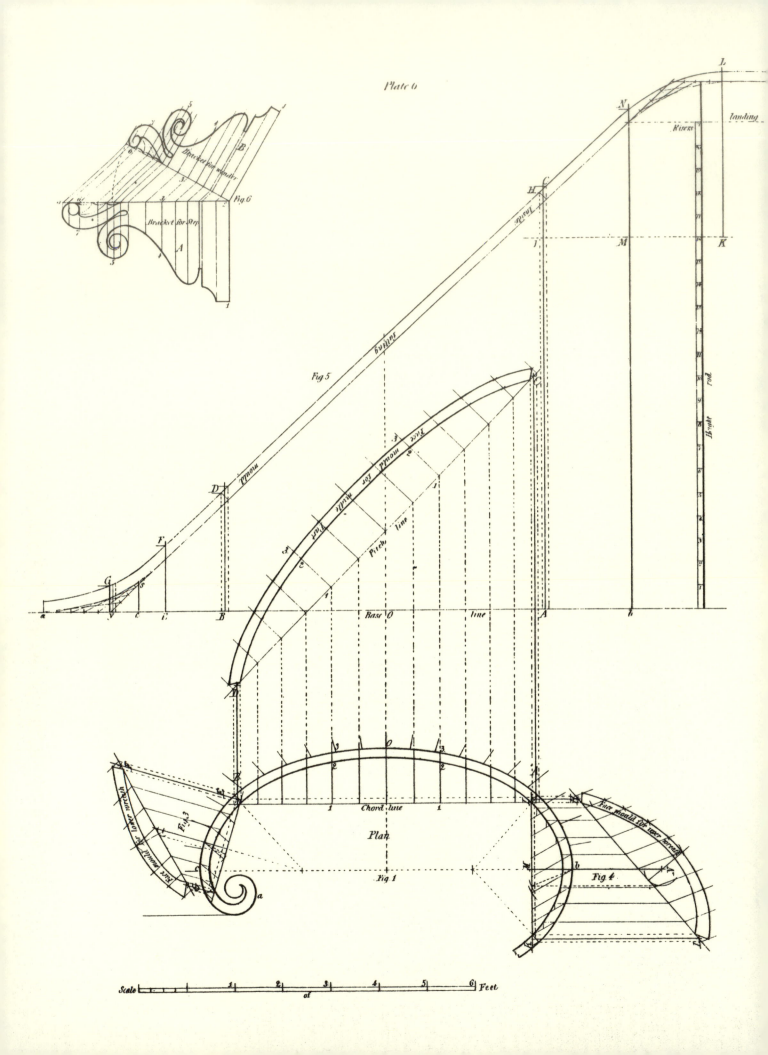

Plate 6

Fig 6

Bracket for winder

B

Bracket for Step

A

L

landing

N

Risers

C

H

Inside

I

M

K

Height rod

Fig 5

railing

mould

D

Face mould for width

F

Pitch line

G

Base O line

A

b

Face mould for upper wreath

Fig 3

Back mould for lower wreath

Chord line

Plan

M

b

Fig 4

Fig 1

a

Scale |⊢⊢⊢⊢⊢⊢|———1———2———3———4———5———6| Feet

of

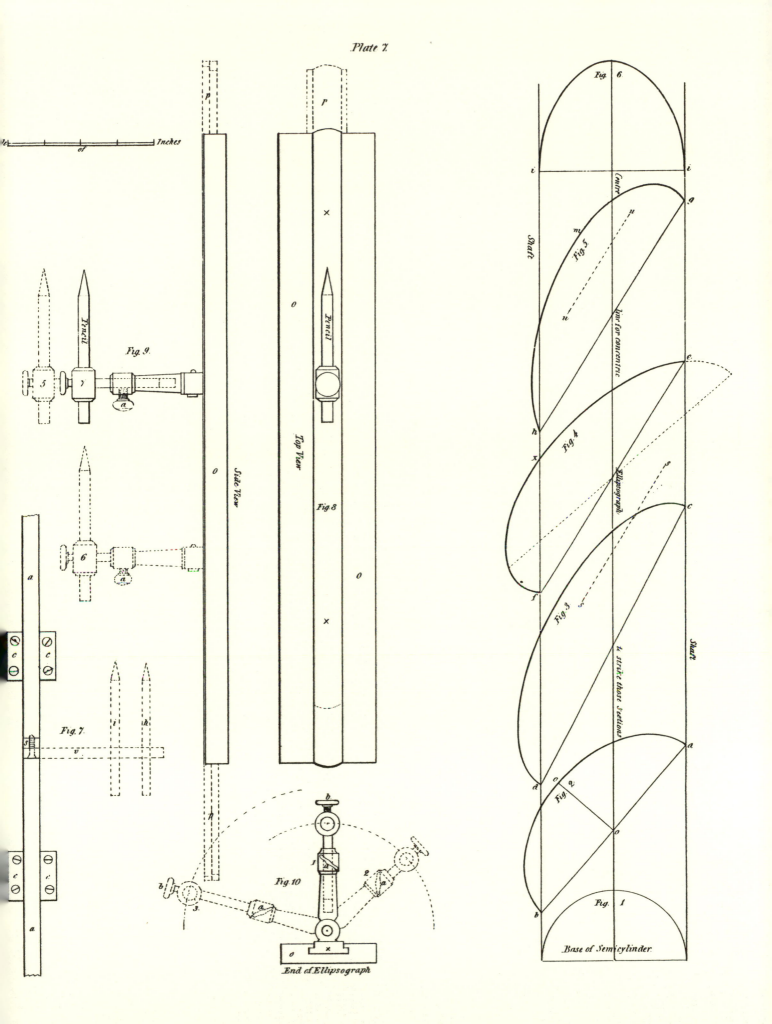

Plate 7.

Inches

Fig. 9.

Pencil

Side View

Top View

Fig. 8

Fig. 7.

Fig. 10

End of Ellipsograph.

Fig. 6

Shaft

Fig. 5

line for concentric

Ellipsograph

Fig. 4

Fig. 3

to strike these sections

Shaft

Fig. 2

Fig. 1

Base of Semicylinder.

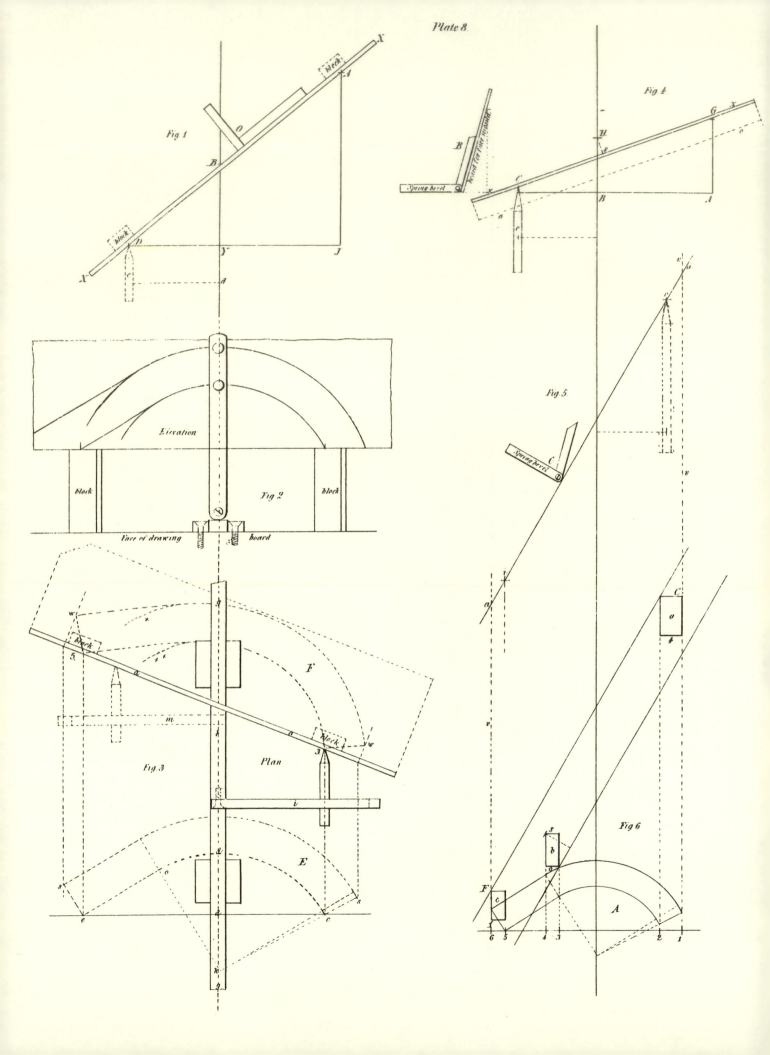

Plate 8.

Fig 1.

block

O

B

block

D

c

X

X

A

d

J

Fig 4.

Spring bevel

B

H

C

x

a

e

G

X

o

B

A

c

Fig 2.

Elevation

block

block

Fig 5.

a

v

v

r

Spring bevel

C

D

Face of drawing   board

w

block

Fig 3.

x

m

a

a

block

Plan

F

s

o

s

e

d

c

k

q

E

Fig 6.

s

b

a

C

o

F

c

A

6 5   4 3   2 1